W9-AGE-633

SAM McAUGHTRY was born in a fiercely loyalist area of Belfast. He became an award-winning *Irish Times* columnist in 1981. He had already achieved popularity as the author of *The Sinking of the Kenbane Head* (Blackstaff Press, 1977) and as a raconteur on the popular RTÉ radio programme *Sunday Miscellany*. He has since gone on to write numerous books. He is a Life Member of the Irish Writer's Union, was named in 1986 as Irish Columnist of the Year, and in 1998 he was awarded an Honorary Doctorate by the National University of Ireland. He is the first person from Northern Ireland to be elected into Seanad Éireann.

On the outside looking in

a memoir

SAM McAUGHTRY

THE
BLACKSTAFF
PRESS
BELFAST

First published in 2003 by
Blackstaff Press Limited
4c Heron Wharf, Sydenham Business Park
Belfast BT3 9LE
with the assistance of
The Arts Council of Northern Ireland

© Sam McAughtry, 2003
All rights reserved

Sam McAughtry has asserted his right under the Copyright, Designs and
Patents Act 1988 to be identified as the author of this work.

Typeset by Techniset Typesetters, Newton-le-Willows, Merseyside

Printed in Ireland by ColourBooks Ltd

A CIP catalogue record for this book is available from the British Library

ISBN 0-85640-736-4

www.blackstaffpress.com

In memory of

Paddy Devlin (1925–1999),

a socialist and a true friend

Preface

This book covers the years 1971 to 2002, the most rewarding period of my life. In the end, some might judge the rewards to be modest enough, but everything is relative. When I was a teenager, my dearest wish was to go to sea as an ordinary seaman, study and become a master mariner. I wanted to achieve this in the lifetimes of my father and my dear brother Mart. They were unskilled engine-room hands, and I used to picture them in the gloomy fo'c'sle of their ship, halfway between Halifax, Nova Scotia, and Belfast, showing my letters to their shipmates, with my name printed at the top of the page, under the name of my command.

In February 1940 I climbed the gangway of Mart's ship to learn that he had spoken up for me and that I could sign on the SS *Kenbane Head* for her next voyage across the Atlantic Ocean. I shook my head in bitter disappointment and told him that, weary of waiting, I had joined the Royal Air Force (RAF) and was to sail to England in two days' time.

As it happened, if I had sailed with Mart I should almost certainly have been lost, along with my cousin Jim Emerson. Their ship was sunk by German shellfire in a famous sea battle in the middle of the Atlantic, and wherever Mart was during the action, I would have been there beside him. Instead of taking command of a ship, I became an RAF officer, attacking German shipping at sea and in harbour.

It was my first book, an account of the sea battle in which my brother was lost and the story of my growing-up years in happy poverty in Belfast, that opened the way for my twenty-five-year love affair with the city of Dublin and its wonderful, outgoing people.

After the war I entered the civil service, and by 1971 I was an active trade unionist, but I was drawn to the top echelon of my union in the beginning only because I wanted to edit a failing monthly magazine. I had for years been writing articles for the Belfast papers, and I was the North Down local government stringer for the papers and for BBC Radio Ulster. All through those years I had been fighting a drink problem which was finally beaten back after a stay in hospital. I was discharged from there in September 1971, and from the day that I walked through that hospital door and on to the bombed streets of Belfast, my life changed completely. The book starts from there.

I could never have guessed the new direction my life would take in 1971. Today, there's a good chance that I would be recognised in any town in Ireland, and greeted with a smile. It's a lovely feeling. This is the story of how it all came about: my days with the *Irish Times*; challenging the Provos by heading up the Peace Train Organisation; becoming the first person from Northern Ireland to win a seat in Seanad Éireann; and, finally, being awarded an honorary doctorate by the National University of Ireland.

I would like to pay tribute to Belfast sound engineer Gerry McCann, whose phone call in 1977 to Maxwell

Sweeney (God be good to him), the then producer of the radio programme *Sunday Miscellany*, inviting him to listen to my first broadcast for RTÉ from the Belfast studio, helped me to form a thousand friendships with the people of the Republic. This allowed me, in turn, to pass the South's liberal views on the North to the working-class unionist people amongst whom I grew up. I hope this memoir will help to advance understanding in this area.

SAM McAUGHTRY
COMBER, COUNTY DOWN
JULY 2003

At Dundonald in County Down there is a park that sits alongside a Norman motte. Beside the park, in the churchyard of St Mary's, self-consciously baroque, is a domed mausoleum, erected in 1842 by the family of the Reverend John Cleland, who made a fortune by informing on the local United Irishmen. With their inheritance his family bought a big house just underneath the Stormont plateau and added bits, in the fashion of the time, to make it look like a castle. Today it is known as Stormont Castle, where British secretaries of state play a game of pretend tug-of-war between the British government and the Irish republican movement, in which the British allow the rope to slip through their fingers, one millimetre at a time, while calling over their shoulders to the unionists not to worry, that the game is even-handed.

In 1971 I used to sit on a seat in this park, hiding from

my colleagues in the civil service, wishing that I could work up the courage to bring my useless life to an end. I'd been two years back on the drink, after seven fruitful years off it. The potential of the disease grows during the dry years, as it waits, ready for a lightning war should the victim's guard drop.

The viciousness of its advance had stripped me of every vestige of pride. In the seven years of sobriety I had done well enough in work and had made a decent contribution to the trade union and Labour movements. I had moved with my wife, Phyllis, and three daughters away from a housing estate when the curse of the 1960s was beginning to show in the behaviour of local teenage boys; we hadn't long settled into a quiet, suburban area when the slip came.

The trigger for a slip hardly ever bears scrutiny: in my case it was the widespread rout of Labour across Northern Ireland in the Stormont and local government elections of 1968. I had written the manifesto and had worked hard and sore for the party in the Castlereagh area, and on the evening when our candidates were blitzed, I went on my own to a football supporters' club, where nobody would know me, and got slowly, quietly and desperately drunk. The fact that the Labour movement all across the United Kingdom was taking a long count didn't register with me: I was sure that I had failed my good friends in our little pocket of politics, that my judgement had proved to be dreadful. The decline started then, to the point that two years later I had absented myself from work, torn up letters unopened, stayed in bed until the house was empty, only to slip out at around 9.30 in the morning to sit on the seat in the park. Down in the bowl of the park I could see children playing on swings. Up on the top of the motte a father was flying a kite for his little girl, just as I had once done. I had now failed my lovely family: they didn't know what it was that made me so silent and withdrawn in the house.

One afternoon in August 1971 I rose from the seat: it was two o'clock, my wife was in her office in Belfast, the people who knew me would be at work. I made my way back to my empty house. When I turned the corner of the avenue I noticed that there was a car outside. As I was putting the key in the front door, two people got out of the car and hailed me. They were from my work. They had come to tell me that it was time I had treatment for my problem.

The treatment lasted six weeks. As well as the family I had visitors from work, but they called only to gaze on the fallen trapeze artist. Towards the end of my stay in the clinic my wife gave me the glad news that our house had been sold and that the deal was done. It had been on the market for a year. It wasn't an excuse for my drinking, but the bridging loan hadn't helped me to cope with it.

Until God calls me I will never forget the final day of the treatment. That's when they gave me the Antabuse. Three of us were being prepared for the experience. We were in good spirits, like army recruits with only one more test to do before leaving boot camp to join our regiments. The drill sergeant nurses were pleasant, smiling, treating us as full-blown soldiers, wishing us luck going into this last run over the toughest assault course of all.

We were looking forward to going home, believing that the treatment and therapy we'd had would keep us sober

for all time. We were laughing and joking and I was
leading the wisecracking when the time came to drink the
hard stuff and take the Antabuse. We were each given a
tablẹt and a generous glass of our favourite brand of
spirits to wash it down. The nurses watched, smiling, as
we drank it. The horsing around really got going then: we
were all three sophisticated comics, reaching effortlessly
for saloon bar stories and anecdotes. I was feeling
euphoric and I soon staked a strong claim as wit of the
ward – the two nurses thought I was hilarious.

We sat on beds that were curtained off into three
cubicles and, as the whiskey got to work, the shouting and
the laughter grew louder. Truth to tell, the whiskey, as
usual, heightened our appreciation of the nurses as
women, and this added to the attraction of the hour.
What a lovely way to end the clinic experience, we
thought. It was like the celebrations after the march-past;
we were metaphorically throwing our hats in the air, as
the American marines did on passing out. In fact, we were
closer than we knew to passing out.

Suddenly the nurses produced hand mirrors and held
them before our eyes: what I saw made my voice die
away. Every trace of drollery faded. My cheeks and
forehead were an angry crimson, in a face that was ugly
and swollen, but the worst features of all were the eyes –
no longer brown, they were swimming in blood. The nurse
saw my reaction and nodded grimly. She was no longer
the patient's friend.

The humiliation that filled me had no need for her
words or glances. At first I thought the nausea that was
growing in me was self-disgust, but a bout of vomiting
made it clear that the whiskey and the Antabuse were at
war. The curtains were drawn around our beds, a kidney

dish was placed on the floor beside each bed, and I fell into a nightmare world of threatening cartoon creatures; I was fleeing from some shapeless horror that was tumbling and rushing over the ground after me. It ended when I awoke with a cry to find the nurse bending over me, swabbing my brow and, to my relief, smiling sympathetically.

When I got up it was to find that the other two had showered and gone. My own shower helped to wash away the squalid seediness of the experience. Over a mug of tea the nurses were most attentive; there were no lectures and nobody warned me of the perils of drink. I was given a little bottle of the Antabuse tablets and advised to take one a day, until I felt no need for their protection.

To a friendly goodbye and an invitation to drop by the clinic as often as I wished, I walked down the stairs and into a late summer street in Belfast, 1971. It was an almost deserted city, where people looked fearfully at oddly parked cars and each city centre plume of smoke or explosion was seen by one side as a military strike, and by the other as an outrage more sectarian by far than the acts which had provoked it. The Antabuse effect was dead by now: my stride lengthened, my shoulders straightened, and I hurried towards the newly structured life that had been offered to me. The house was sold, my debts would soon be paid, and I would soon be able to gather my scattered family around me again and make a fresh start.

The solicitor was in his forties, good-looking, tall, athletic. His secretary was leaning over his shoulder from behind.

They both looked up as I knocked. There seemed to be a closeness between them. I asked him when I could expect the cheque from the sale of the house. 'When it's ready,' he said, curtly. The girl looked excited at his brio.

'My wife tells me that you have already paid the estate agent,' I said.

'What of it?'

'It's just that I would like to pay the bills myself.'

The solicitor took a different view. His eyes narrowed, he sat forward in his chair and jabbed a finger at me.

'Look, mister, I've seen your file. There's a second mortgage on your house. You are in money trouble. You've just come out of the clinic for drink. I've paid the estate agent because, if it had been left to you, they mightn't have seen their money. All right?'

The second mortgage I had arranged with a money-lender. There's a story in the margin here: when I turned up to collect the money, I found the moneylender and his secretary under attack by a man whose house had been put up for sale after his payments fell behind. The man was standing on the counter throwing acid from a bottle at both victims and I could see the smoke rising from their clothes. I tackled the man and held him while the police and an ambulance were called. I had stopped the attack in time and they were only slightly injured. My trouble provided their rescue. Life is strange.

At Alcoholics Anonymous they warn you not to hold resentment because it could lead to a slip. I smiled at the solicitor. I liked resentment. Without it I would have been living on a loyalist housing estate, feeling no shame for my drinking, regarding it as a part of macho living. Along with the humiliation that had attended my drinking, there had still been resentment at the mock sympathy from those who had come to view me in the hospital, the *Schadenfreude* so evident in their eyes. There was no way that I could reply to this solicitor and keep my dignity: I would have to get used to this treatment. But the resentment I felt wasn't negative: it was healing. I was partway ready now for the rest of the challenge, when I must face the ordeal of returning to work.

The two heads were together again as I left the solicitor's office. Back on the city street I took in a deep breath of Belfast air. There was a strong smell of burning office block in it, but at least, so far, my cheque had survived the holocaust.

Phyllis was living with her mother in her house near Cave Hill. The weather was beautiful. The next morning I walked to the base of the hill and lay down with the morning sun on my face. Cave Hill was where I had played as a boy; it was over these slopes that my lovely brother Mart and I had walked greyhounds for a fee of a few shillings from an owner who lived in nearby Henderson's Avenue. I was ten and Mart was seventeen. He was my hero and my protector against the thumps and slaps I got from my other brother, Jack, who was ten years older than me. It seemed to irritate Jack that I was forever hanging around the house with a book, in the years when I was, as we used to say, 'delicate', taking duck eggs, Angiers Emulsion, and goat's milk to build myself up. 'Why don't you go out to the street and play like other kids?' Jack used to shout, and when I grew stronger that's what I was to do – in spades. I became a ringleader, with more nerve than the other kids, and when I got into trouble for it, more thumps followed. That's when Mart wasn't around. He wasn't around now, for good. He was dead, killed-in-action, gone.

When he was out of work, walking greyhounds and training our school soccer team for another half-crown, Mart listened to my tall tales and pretended to believe them, and when I grew tired he carried me on his back up the steeper slopes of Cave Hill. Now, lying on the grass with my eyes closed, gradually there came over me a peace that I hadn't known for many years, not even in the seven years when I'd been dry, for any gains made in that time had been achieved in a mood of fierce ambition, a wild energy, following a course that had no sensible destination, with, too often, a disregard for others. There would be a pattern to my life from now on. Whatever I proposed to do with the time left to me would be done to a plan, and, whichever way it went, writing would be central to it. I expected a smug and unforgiving reaction from some of the walking coat-hangers around me in the ministry, but, as they say in AA, all things pass.

I hired a caravan at Millisle, on the seaward shoulder of the Ards Peninsula, and Phyllis and the three girls moved in while we looked for a house. The days that followed were marvellously restful. The girls travelled to school by bus, Phyllis took the car to work, and I was happy to find a place along the seashore and just sit, looking across to the thin outline of the Scottish coast, and relax. It was natural that I should have compared my stillness, as I sat by the beach at Millisle, to the long days that I had spent on the seat in the park: Millisle was therapeutic, the other was like stasis, the stoppage of the system's lifeblood.

I was going to have to go back to work, and it wasn't

going to be pleasant, but it was easy to put this thought away until nearer the event. In the evenings we would all go to one of Millisle's seaside cafés for a meal, and later play table tennis in the games room on site, and end the day sitting in the cosy caravan, telling tales, enjoying the luxury of being a family once again. My daughters didn't know how much pleasure I was taking just in seeing them so close to me, after the months I'd spent ashamed to face them. I didn't go into confessional mode – it doesn't sit easily on Ulstermen. A somewhat nasty couple of years had run their course and the future was what mattered. As one week gave way to the next, I was getting the familiar feeling that there were things I wanted to do: the first of these was that I wanted to write my way out of the past. In hospital I had spent a full and rewarding day with the psychiatrist. I knew what to avoid. There would be no more overturning of icons: I knew now my limitations.

Phyllis and I went house-hunting, and on the very first day we found the house in Comber that we still live in today. It's just a standard semi-detached house and I swear often at its pokiness, even with just the two of us there. I could be doing with twice the space, and I could comfortably have bought something bigger, but this is a lucky house: everything that's nice in my life has happened since I moved in and I wouldn't change it even if I won the lottery.

On the way to my first day back at work, after a three-month absence, I had to pass the park. On a sudden impulse I swung the car off the road and into a quiet avenue opposite. I parked, walked up the hill, and sat on the seat. In truth, I wanted to see how differently I felt from the last time I'd occupied the seat, but I told myself that the little break would settle my nerves, and it was true that I was jumpy. Going into the huge building was going to be no treat. Being meek and mild and paying dues to society didn't sit easily on me. I sat, taking deep breaths of the clean, fresh morning air, and looked around me. Down below, in the bowl of the park, tiny tots were being gently pushed on the swings by their minders. The roar of the traffic on the road outside had reduced to a low murmur. Here in this peaceful place I closed my eyes and called the roll. I was sound in wind and limb; my brain was clear; I had enough money from the equity on the house to clear all my debts and have a bit over; my family were around me and we had moved into a new house in a new area; the next few days would be troublesome, even humiliating – alcoholism is a disease that is assumed by most people to be a character defect, a point made most strongly by those who have real character defects – but this would pass. As a former editor of a union journal with a ten thousand-strong circulation I had, within a year, turned it around from less than half that figure, made it pay its way, and seen it quoted in the Belfast dailies, but all of this hadn't been achieved without making enemies. Still, thank God, if I needed help there were people in the hospital willing to offer it. It was a statement of account that would have been well beyond my wildest dreams the last time I had sat on this seat.

A man appeared around the bend of the narrow path that led past the seat. On seing me, he waved. He was Bill, an ex-regular army officer, on a pension. His drink problem was far worse than mine. I had spent time with him in our local, and we had even sat together on this seat, sometimes waiting for the pub on the road behind us to open. Bill's system was so saturated with drink that he used to crumple over the table after about four glasses of wine. The pleasure that his company gave, for he was a most intelligent and entertaining man, was no kind of recompense for the embarrassment that his almost instantaneous collapse caused.

'Is it yourself?' I called. I could see he'd had one already before leaving the house, the glitter in his eyes gave it away. Bill liked to go out for a bracing walk before passing out in the pub. God knows, he was deceptive in appearance, a tall, straight-shouldered man in his fifties, dressed in tweeds, a checked shirt and hand-made shoes. He had a lovely young wife and three children. When he came out of the army in the early 1970s, he'd been placed first in a UK-wide fast-track civil service exam, but he was now out of the service, medically unfit.

'The place is full of rumours about you,' he said, looking at me with his keen eyes. 'They say you went into hospital to avoid a debt summons.'

There was an erroneous impression amongst boozers that if a debtor went into the drink clinic, the summons server from the civil court was not allowed past the door.

'I have been taking the six-week course at the clinic,' I said, 'I'm on Antabuse. I'm sitting here dreading going back to work this morning.'

'There's no doubt about it,' Bill said, sitting on the edge of the seat, 'you tramped on a good many corns with the union mag and in your newspaper campaign.' He was talking about my role in helping to abolish the marriage bar in the civil service and banking, by which girls had to leave their jobs on marriage. This practice was insisted upon by the unions, not the management. I had cut the tripes out of many a fellow trade unionist in the campaign. 'There'll be many a one glad to see you levelled,' Bill went on. 'How do you feel about staying dry?'

I told him that I felt good about it. 'I know now why I broke down, last time.'

'You're lucky.' He gave a wry little smile. 'You'll be able to fill the vacuum.'

'I hope so,' I said. 'I'm going to write as soon as I feel able.'

'You know I wish you well,' he said.

I sat, watching him leave. He would be there at the bar as the doors opened. He'd be the butt of sniggers from the housing estate drinkers, but for the present his walk was upright, his clothes sat neatly on him, and for the short time left to his manners and dignity that morning, he was someone well worth knowing.

I got up to go. The way ahead wasn't going to be nice, but things could have been one hell of a lot worse.

The principal officer had sent word to me in hospital that I would have his full support and understanding and he wished me well. His full support and understanding took thirty seconds of his time when, at 9.15, he summoned me from my desk: 'I'm sorry, but I'm afraid I've had to replace you. I think that your next step is to go to the establishment officer, and he will tell you where you'll be going next.'

The principal officer was an Englishman, a remote academic, who had hardly met me during the two years I'd been in his division. When he had finished delivering his message he sat staring at me, smiling frostily. I felt as though I was back in the RAF, being dressed down by a ground staff officer. This man knew nothing at all about me, except that I was expendable. I almost saluted before turning and leaving his office. This was how it was going to be, I thought, and I'd better get used to it. I had just paid another instalment of the drink tab.

The establishment officer knew me well. I had met him many times in the line of trade union duty. There are times in union negotiations when stones are turned up that reveal hiccups on management's part and it is a measure of the union representative's character as to the use he chooses to make of the information. I had had the respect of the establishment officer in this regard, and, in return, I had found him to be decent and even-handed. I expected civility from him and it was there in good measure. 'You're a good worker,' he said. 'If you weren't an economic proposition, you wouldn't be back here.'

I was transferred to a branch that had been run by a woman whose notions of supervision were Dickensian. Files were heaped on the desk, on the floor and on the window ledges. Her immediate subordinate had been on sick leave for several months and her desk, opposite the staff officer's, was in the same sorry state. Nearly every letter issued by the staff of the office had had to be vetted twice before issue. This cross-checking was at the heart of the untidiness. I was feeling too knocked about to be delighted, but I was certainly pleased to see this mess. I love to clear up clutter. It gives me great satisfaction to put a shine where it's been. When I was a boy at home, I used to volunteer to scrub the stone tiles of the kitchen floor, for the pleasure it gave me to see the floor cloth restore the colour and character of each individual tile. I still do the dishes at home, and the messier the saucepans the better. Before we got the central heating in, when Phyllis was working, I used to rise well before her, clean out the fire, empty the cinders, lay a new one, and wash the hearth. (I mentioned this once while visiting Paddy and Teresa

Devlin and I saw the look of amazement on Teresa's face. 'Thanks very much,' Paddy said later. 'With one blow you've shaken the foundations of a marriage that has lasted the guts of fifty years. I have never washed a dish in my life, nor brushed a floor. You're putting our friendship under a terrible strain.')

By lunchtime I was feeling more confident. The staff in the office numbered about twenty, and I knew that they were peeping at me from under bent heads, wondering. I stayed at my desk, spoke only to two of the junior line managers and tried to make sense of the jumble of papers all over the place. As I walked down the office on my way to the restaurant on the top floor, I caught the eyes of one or two of the clerks, gave them a friendly smile, and saw it returned. In the restaurant I spotted a group of colleagues from my old post and I carried my plate from the counter and joined them. I was nervous, but this was the only way to handle it.

As usual, they were solving all the main political and social problems of the North, taking care to trim their own ideas to fit in with those of the most senior officer present. I joined in the chat and was glad that there was no strain or tension. As I rose to leave, with two others, I felt good: apart from the first few minutes of the working day, things were going nicely. I even wondered why I had been so fearful of this first day.

At the top of the stairs I left the other two to buy cigarettes at the little shop by the wall. This done, I took the stairs two at a time and turned into the corridor, ending up two steps behind my lunch companions. I was in time to hear one say to the other, 'I wonder if he'll stay dry.' I dropped back quietly, looked for an escape, and turned into a Gents. They walked on with their heads together. I looked in the mirror and gave a wry smile. 'How are things?' I asked. 'As well as can be expected,' said the face in the mirror.

Clearing the office work would take months. I couldn't think of a better therapy. The union work and the Labour Party activities would be thinned down drastically and in the evenings I would resume writing the good-humoured pieces for the northern newspapers that had given me so much pleasure before my slip. Some time in the future I would make a start on something more substantial.

There were several letters waiting for me. One was from the general secretary of the union, wishing me success on my 'uphill climb'. Three cheers for trade union clichés: is there any other sort of climb?

The political events of 1972 made that year whiz by at a furious rate. This was the year that direct rule was imposed on Northern Ireland by Edward Heath, and it was the year that settled in my mind for all time the realisation that the people and the government in Britain were light years away from regarding unionists as anything other than a bloody nuisance, too blinkered and stupid to realise that they were as Irish as the IRA bombers. The activity that followed the British takeover of Stormont was an eye-opener: the staff at the Northern Ireland Office moved into specially built prefab huts, around which were erected security measures aimed at no one but Northern Irish civil servants. We were suspect. I felt like an Indian under colonial rule. In particular, the junior ministers brought over with the Secretary of State were an undistinguished lot, most of whom would never have been considered for any kind of high office at Westminster. I recall, when Labour took government in Britain shortly after the establishment of direct rule, hearing a senior Northern Irish civil servant relate how his minister, a one-time ship's engineer, kept reaching for maritime engineering parallels as he wrestled with the problems of agriculture. One bright spot in the picture was the increase in promotion opportunities for some of my colleagues, who were needed to do the secondary jobs in the over-staffed private offices, while British civil servants did the real thinking. One incoming Labour minister being shown around the building was brought in to meet me. He asked me, eagerly, when he would be presenting the organisers of a ministry egg-laying competition with their government grant. 'It's all right,' I told him, to his evident disappointment, 'we post it out.'

Today, the one thing that I do remember about the dozens of Westminster MPs and leaping lords who were given junior roles in Northern Ireland all the way through direct rule is that, although some received knighthoods and peerages, not one gained any kind of high political standing on returning to Britain. I used to think that William Whitelaw, the first Secretary of State, was first class, until the news broke at the end of 2002 about his alleged collusion with Cardinal Conway in covering up the involvement of a Catholic priest in the bombing of Claudy and the killing of nine people in July 1972.

Prior to direct rule, I used to liken our unionist politicians to the Maltese, who, at one time, also waved the union flag, felt proud of the pounding they had taken from the Nazis in a just war, and looked to Westminster to help them over sticky economic patches as a reward for their suffering. Much good it did the Maltese. Despite their pleas, they were never a part of Britain's long-term plans, and when it suited the Foreign Office, Britain left Malta with a brutal unemployment problem, due to the closure of their naval shipyard facilities, but gave them the George Cross for their trouble. When I was active in the Northern Ireland Labour Party I used to put this point to unionist MPs, like Jim Kilfedder and Harold McCusker, two of the more liberal thinkers in the party, but both waved away my warnings: 'We have friends at Westminster who are very powerful,' I was told. The scene at Stormont after direct rule didn't seem to bear this out to me; unionists today know it, and they now hold on to the consent clause in the Good Friday Agreement as a lifebelt, where once they assumed that consent was the whole ship.

The Royal Ulster Constabulary (RUC) took its share of suffering. I hope that the unionists have grasped the significance of the George Cross that was accepted recently by the Chief Constable. I wonder what the British will award to Gibraltar, when the time comes to put the union flags away there. Mention of the 'Spanish dimension' has already been made.

But all that I did in 1972 was to note this. As the year went out and another year came in I kept busy, turning out good work for the ministry, as well as writing articles in the evenings for the *Belfast Telegraph* and the *News Letter*. One or two of these pieces were causing eyebrows to rise in the corridors of Dundonald House, where I worked, for some were appearing in the pink business pages. I had been poking fun at the new jargon in management memos, like *Please let me have, by close of play . . .* or *We'll kick for touch on this one, gentlemen*. I had pointed out that nine times out of ten the managers who used these sporting expressions wouldn't have known whether a ball was blown up or stuffed and that those civil servants who used such expressions had lifted them in the first place from correspondence sent by their Westminster counterparts. Indeed, our solicitors and parliamentary draughtsmen were much more creative in the language of their notes to administrators. In this regard I found, surprisingly, that I had a liking for the discipline of making statutory rules and orders in council. With tricky legislation, it was like sending the brain for a sauna.

As 1973 came and went I kept my head down, running a ministry branch that was ticking over nicely. In the evenings I would write articles for the papers and I was attempting, gradually, to take the writing further, into territory that was new to me. Working into the small hours, I would compose long essays on all sorts of subjects, in order to teach myself the discipline of writing to a standard beyond that of light journalism.

It was towards the end of 1973 that I went to my last annual union conference. The hall was full of new faces. Seated at the back of the audience I watched and listened, as anonymous as a first-time delegate, and the evenings were spent, not being smart in the hotel bar, as in the old days, but walking by the seafront, alone. On the last day of the conference I offered to speak to a motion, and when I reached the microphone the president and general secretary smiled and greeted me most kindly. I received a nice reception from the audience. It was a fond way to say goodbye as a union activist. An even more satisfying development was to come later, when I was awarded the gold medal of the Northern Ireland Public Service Alliance, a union which has seen two of its general secretaries hold the presidency of the Irish Congress of Trade Unions. With Brendan Harkin and Bill Hodges in the mid-1960s, I had worked to overcome unionist resistance to, and gain membership of, the Irish Congress of Trade Unions. We also achieved equal pay for women in the 60s, but my proudest moment came in the 70s, when the infamous marriage bar, the practice of sacking women on marriage, which I had opposed for years, was abolished.

Within the space of three months at the end of 1973 and into 1974, I had requests from the literary editors of both Belfast papers asking me for more of the same. My writing seemed to have taken a turn for the better. Another thing: both editors wanted to meet me. This is a rare privilege, and it carries with it the inference of higher fees, something that hurts literary editors like third-degree burns. In the circumstances it seemed to me that it was time to get down, at last, to the book. Everything in my life was looking good. Because of my hard work and low profile, the novelty value of my breakdown had sunk below the gossip horizon. I had even been promoted to deputy principal, although the announcement was held up because at least two principal officers refused to take me as their deputy, because of what they regarded as my lack of respect for rank. I was amused to learn that it was Jimmy Young, the ministry's permanent secretary, who had cleared my promotion. 'He's his own man,' he was reported as saying. Since then I've been honoured in a number of ways, but that vote of confidence did more for me than many of the others. As we used to say in the war, I wouldn't have called the King my uncle!

The subject of my first book was to be the naval action in which my brother Mart lost his life. An excellent account of the battle was written by George Pollock and published by William Kimber of London in 1958. A convoy of thirty-eight ships, designated HX 84, left Halifax, Nova Scotia, on 20 October 1940, for the UK. My brother's ship, the *Kenbane Head*, one of the Ulster Steamship Company's freighter fleet, was part of the convoy. She had a crew of forty, mostly Belfastmen, but including some seamen from the Irish Free State. Unknown to the British Admiralty, a German heavy cruiser, the *Admiral Scheer*, had broken the blockade in the Denmark Strait and had penetrated the convoy lanes.

Owing to the wide-ranging demands on the Royal Navy, the only protection provided for the convoy came from an old passenger liner, the *Jervis Bay*, which had been pressed into service as an auxiliary cruiser. It was one of a fleet normally used to monitor enemy warship movements or to intercept ships carrying the enemy's war materials. Six-inch guns had been fitted to the *Jervis Bay*'s deck, but for fighting purposes her hull might as well have been made of cardboard. Her captain, Fogarty Fegen, was a Royal Navy captain brought out of retirement. He was born in Chatham, the son of an admiral who came from Tipperary. When, in the late afternoon of 5 November, the outline of the *Admiral Scheer* appeared on the north-east horizon, the convoy was only halfway across the North Atlantic. It was then that Fegen dropped smoke floats, steered for the enemy, opened fire, and ordered the convoy to scatter.

The *Jervis Bay*'s six-inch guns were no match for the armament of the so-called 'pocket battleship'. In the ensuing slaughtering match the *Jervis Bay* was reduced to a flaming wreck, but Fegen had gained vital time for the ships of the convoy. By the time he died with 189 of his crew, darkness had fallen. Thirty-three ships escaped with their sorely needed cargoes. Captain Fegen was awarded a posthumous Victoria Cross for his bravery, but Mart's ship, the *Kenbane Head*, was sunk with the loss of twenty of the forty crewmen on board. Killed with Mart was Jim Emerson, our cousin, on his first trip. Mart first went to sea when I was a lad of thirteen and from that time I had always written long letters to him. He was no great correspondent himself, but he told me that he loved my letters and used to read them aloud to his shipmates in the fo'c'sle, in places like St John's, New Brunswick, Philadelphia, Boston, Montreal and Quebec. The book that I was to begin in 1974 was to be a memorial to him.

*

I had very little cooperation from the Ulster Steamship Company regarding the firm's records of the war. I was told that a fire caused by terrorists had destroyed most of these, but I fancy they were anxious to keep quiet about the conditions under which their seamen worked. In any case, I wasn't worried about this at first. I was having a most fascinating time studying the maritime history of the war, especially the period leading up to November 1940. At school I had detested history but now, in the specific area that interested me, I couldn't get enough of it. I spent hours in the evenings reading accounts of German surface raiders, the U-boat war, and the British auxiliary cruisers. Through my links with retired merchant navy ratings I collected personal stories from these men, who, unlike members of the armed forces, were true volunteers, working for disgracefully low wages and living in even more disgraceful shipboard conditions. They could have stayed ashore after pay-off on completion of any voyage, yet, in their thousands, they signed on again and again, and went to face the unspeakable terrors of sudden attacks from submarines, mines, aircraft or surface raiders. In the armed forces medals were glinting everywhere, but the merchant navy heroes were not only barely recognised in this area, they were not even regarded officially as combatants until the very scale of their losses forced the war department to extend to the merchant navy the on-shore privileges enjoyed by the uniformed forces.

My brother's pay stopped on the day that he died. So did Jim Emerson's. This was the policy in the British merchant service. My trade union profile might have been one of the reasons why, so long after the war, the Ulster Steamship Company didn't welcome my approaches. But this was 1974, the year of the loyalist putsch, or, as they preferred to put it, the Ulster Workers' Strike.

I was never prevented from going to work when the barricades went up in May, because I knew nearly all of the Ulster Defence Association (UDA) men who manned them. As the local newspaper correspondent I had some kind of standing in the neighbourhood, but not everyone was so well placed. The UDA was particularly obtuse where public service workers were concerned, so I wasn't surprised when one of my clerks rang up to report that the UDA men in the village where he lived on the Ards Peninsula were stopping him from driving to work. Sure enough, I could hear the sound of flutes and drums in the background, so I assured the young man that his absence was in order. Later, when things had returned to abnormal, and the permanent secretaries of all the departments in the civil service had bowed before the threat of the UDA to fight with sewage on the streets, on the beaches and that they would never surrender, and the Sunningdale government fell, we all declared that never before had so much of a stench been threatened to so many by so few. It was at this time that I learned from a girl who lived in the same village as the clerk that, far from having to give way to force, he had been a leading light on the barricades, and a leading flautist in the band.

Before I could question him, however, he was lifted by the army, together with the entire platoon to which he belonged, and lodged in the Maze prison. He was one of a great many loyalist urban guerrillas to learn that their neighbours were not very good at absorbing paramilitaries into their communities and protecting them from arrest. The best-laid plans of the terrorists were leaked almost as soon as they were laid. A short time after his trial and imprisonment, I had a letter from him, enquiring whether his civil service pension rights would continue throughout his gaol sentence.

In the years that followed he studied in the Maze for an Open University degree, on release he took a PhD in conflict studies, and there followed a highly successful career spent in showing Americans around Ulster's hot spots and helping them, no doubt, to take degrees in conflict resolution as well. It was better than bang bang.

The Workers' Strike was enthusiastically supported in the town where I live. As in other loyalist areas, it was not the power-sharing but the all-Ireland consultative commitment that the unionist people rejected. The ordinary people weren't to know then that the loyalist takeover of vital services would result immediately afterwards in the transfer to Britain of army, navy and RAF installations from the North, at a cost of thousands of jobs.

We non-combatants were required to go to the Orange Hall and make our cases for petrol vouchers to UDA majors and captains. When my turn came the captain handling my case studied my surname, then he mentioned one of my daughters: 'Are you her father?' he asked. I nodded. The captain beamed. 'You can have as much petrol as you like,' he said, signing my docket. 'She's a real cracker, so she is.'

Those nights must have been terrifying for the young couple living next door to me. They were Catholics, with a baby only a few weeks old. The UDA knew about them, but no harm came to them during the strike. I brought them loaves and milk, to save them from having to attend at the Orange Hall. When the strike ended the family left, and I remember hoping that they would find as nice a scenic locality as Comber, and wouldn't have to join the vast numbers of Catholics who, after 1969, found themselves back in the cramped city streets that they'd imagined were behind them, as they tried to integrate with Protestants in the liberal 1960s.

When the lights came on again and my writing resumed, it was clear that it would be a long slog to get the necessary material for the naval part of my book. I spoke to survivors and to the relatives of those lost in the action, and made friendships that were to last for life. There was a nine-month hiatus when the book lay waiting for necessary technical details regarding the *Kenbane Head* herself, then, to my delight, I traced a retired captain, Errol Black, who had been a one-time master of the *Kenbane Head* and knew all of her features. Furthermore, he had a complete record of the history of the Ulster Steamship Company going back to the time it was formed by Gustavus Heyn at the turn of the twentieth century. Another amazing break came when, during a visit to the clinic where I had been treated, I met a patient who turned out to be the son of one of the *Kenbane Head*'s deck officers. He was able to give me precious documentary evidence of the battle as seen from the little ship, contained in the report to the Admiralty submitted by Captain Milner, master of the *Kenbane Head*. I then sent a summary of the story to the publishers William Kimber, in London, who liked it.

It was a strange feeling to have written a publishable book. It represented two years' work and a thirty-year dream. Upon submission I had a reaction that was to become familiar to me in the years to come: the word from the publisher expressing interest in the book was enough, without the actual publication. I had proved that I could do it, the rest was routine. However, it was then that I realised I had only written half a book.

Looking at the pages of typescript, it dawned on me that all I had done was write an account of a battle, putting the reader on to the deck of a little cargo ship. I hadn't expressed all of my feelings for Mart, and, worse than that, I hadn't even mentioned my mother, who had lost four of her ten children, the youngest eleven months and the oldest four years when they died. She'd borne that burden and brought up the remaining six of us in the Church of Ireland, without a man to give her comfort in the fiercest burning of her tears. Harry was the youngest to die. Mother had put him to bed and had gone down to the yard to do the washing. After the usual quarter of an hour she climbed the stairs to where Harry, Betty, Jim and myself all shared a bedroom. She found little Harry hanging dead with his nightdress caught on the brass knob of the bedpost. He had climbed to his feet and tried to walk on the bed. I would have been about three then. I still carry the memory of the fuss in the bedroom, and of seeing a strange man in a raincoat. He could have been a policeman.

I had often wondered if my family background carried a story worth the telling. We in the breed took it a good deal for granted, but we were not run-of-the-mill. My mother was the product of a mixed marriage: her father was Catholic and her mother was Protestant. They solved that problem in those days by bringing the daughters up in the faith of the mother and the boys in the faith of the father, so I had three Catholic uncles, lots of Catholic cousins, and two Protestant aunts. Yet my mother and father were pro-British, we lived in a fiercely loyalist area, and in 1935 one of my Catholic uncles was burned out of his house. I was there in the crowd, a schoolboy, excited to hear that a Fenian was being burned out, only to find that it was my poor Uncle Thomas, a dock labourer, who used to give the children pennies when he came home, full of beer, singing, up the street.

My mother loved her brothers dearly and they loved her. My uncles visited us regularly, and so I heard Catholic talk of Christian Brothers, who used the leather tawse where our schoolmasters used the cane, and men's con-fraternities, and of visiting missionaries from the west of Ireland who shouted temperance messages from the pulpit of St Patrick's Chapel, on Donegall Street, where my mate Herbie Beattie had won my highest admiration for going into the church porch, dipping his hand into the holy water font and emerging safely to show me his wet palm. We both tasted it and it was nothing special. Through my Uncle James I knew that it was a lot of rubbish for the men of our street to say that the Catholics wanted to chase Protestants out of Ireland, because that would mean Uncle James wanting to chase his sister and his nephews out.

And weren't there stories fit for a book in a family whose father who went away to sea for three months at a time? On the first afternoon of his homecoming he took Mother out and spent part of his pay-off money buying something stupid for the house, like the first washing machine to appear in Cosgrave Street. You filled this big tank full of water which had been heated in buckets on the gas stove, then you worked a handle on the top, backwards and forwards, until you nearly went crazy with the boredom of it. At the heel of the hunt the clothes weren't washed anything like the way Mother did them in the tub in the scullery, rubbing and scrubbing them on the washboard with hands that had the skin burned beyond repair by the caustic in the soap.

Another one of Dad's great ideas was to buy the first gramophone in Cosgrave Street that could handle up to ten records at a time. The neighbours crowded in to see it in action, but Mother used to sigh that she would far rather have had the money that these gadgets cost, although she loved Dad too much to tell him so. The washing machine lay rusting in the back yard, but the gramophone was used over and over again, I have to admit that.

On the first evening of his arrival, Dad would have two or three of his shipmates in our wee kitchen, and from upstairs in bed we would hear the accents of Dublin, Waterford, Cork and Dundalk. There would be laughter and singing, and we would hold our breaths when Mother sang, in case she fluffed:

> Do you remember sweet Alice, Ben Bolt,
> Sweet Alice whose eyes were so brown?
> She wept with delight when you gave her a smile,
> And trembled with fear at your frown.

A right bastard, Ben Bolt, we agreed upstairs. Then it was my turn to do my act. I would be brought down from bed, my hand in Mother's, and standing in my nightdress I would recite the Ten Commandments to loud applause. Silver money would be pressed into my hand and I would kiss all present. Mother would lead me back upstairs and at the turn of the landing she would lift me in her arms, take the silver money and give me a penny and a goodnight kiss. This suited me fine, for the kisses and applause were reward enough, and I was the one who had been picked to perform, out of the whole family.

As I sat alone in the small hours, looking at the publisher's letter, the family stories were pushing and shoving each other to get out of my head and on to the page. I was what they called 'delicate'. After little Betty died at four years of age from whooping cough, and we had kissed her cold face, I developed rheumatic fever, growing pains, and swollen neck glands. I was certainly very ill, for I remember at about the age of five sleeping day and night on the sofa, with Mother near me, wetting my lips. Two memories are sharp and clear: I was asleep and through the sleep I heard music. I woke up, and it was coming from the radio: Dublin Athlone and Cork was the station, later to become Radio Telefís Éireann (RTÉ), and the music, though I didn't know it then, was Debussy's *Prélude à l'après-midi d'un faune*. Opening my eyes, I remember feeling terribly frightened at the power of the music, the drawn-out, sobbing passages. Mother ran in from the hall when she heard me cry, and when she said that it was a bad dream I didn't argue, although I am convinced that, when I had heard the music through my sleep, I was near to death. Since then, as a guest on a dozen different request radio programmes, I have asked for Debussy's beautiful prelude to be included, and, where the rest of the world associates this piece with pastoral serenity, I still remember the time when Mother, as she told me later, prayed hard and long that God, having taken four of her children, would let her keep this one.

Another memory that I have from those times is of holding Mother's hand in the street as neighbouring women looked at me, pursed their lips, and talked about me as if I wasn't there: 'Have you tried goat's milk, missus?'

'I have, God knows, missus, and the raw duck eggs, and beef tea, and the Angiers Emulsion, and the cod liver oil, and extract of malt.'

'Hm ...' Narrowing the eyes: 'There's not a pick on him. Have you tried taking him to the gasworks? They say there's stuff there you breathe in and it's great for the lungs.'

In Carnmoney cemetery Mother sat tidying up the grave of her four lost children. The wind was bitterly cold, sweeping down from Cave Hill, and I shivered and whimpered. Mother took the fur from round her neck and put it round mine. It helped, but I didn't like the little dry nose and the glass eyes staring up at me. Mother lifted me and carried me the quarter of a mile up the steep Carnmoney hill to the bus, and the whole way there I kept one hand over the eyes of the fox to hide them away from me.

It had taken me two years to write the story of the battle yet it took exactly two months to set down the story of my family, to describe my love for Mart, to pay tribute to my mother, and to put on record the poverty that had crushed the people of Tiger's Bay, where I was brought up. Those were the days of pawnshops and moneylenders: days when the soft-hearted man in the pork store threw a real rasher of ham into an order for bacon ends, to make the gravy that made a meal of dip bread and frizzled bacon ends for seven people, the four dead ones out of the count.

There was humour in the writing, too. I broke up the story of the battle and inserted chapters about Belfast that described my growing-up years. I wrote and asked Ludovic Kennedy, the author, broadcaster, historian and ex-naval officer, to read the manuscript, and he came back in a surprisingly short time with a foreword, from which the following is taken:

> There have been many books about personal wartime experiences, but this one is different. It tells of the author's childhood in a 'two-up, two-down' in North Belfast, of the home from which the father and later his adored brother set out and returned after long spells at sea ... I like the way in which Mr McAughtry follows one chapter on life at home with another on the course of the war in the Atlantic. It is only at the end, when brother Mart is in the convoy attacked by the *Admiral Scheer*, that the two worlds meet ... And in his descriptions of school and family life in pre-war Belfast he proves himself a natural story-teller.

Ludovic Kennedy liked the book. I said it to myself a hundred times.

In late 1977, while the book was with the publisher, the Troubles hadn't left my family untouched. My daughter was married to a prison officer, and the IRA, and the loyalists to a much lesser extent, were murdering prison officers. In this year Desmond Irvine, the latest one to be assassinated, was shot in the head by the IRA as he left the offices of my union, in Wellington Park, Belfast. I was full of praise for the courage shown by Roddy, my son-in-law, and his colleagues in these times.

Mostly it was his dad who drove Roddy to his duties at Crumlin Road gaol, but several times I was happy to stand in. The first time I did so was in the aftermath of the killing of two of Roddy's colleagues as they came out of their social club in Langley Street, opposite the gaol, one lunchtime. Roddy had almost joined them for lunch on that occasion, but he was called away at the last minute.

The menacing evening emptiness of the route began at Lower Donegall Street; it became more and more dangerous when the junction with North Queen Street was reached, for this was the heart of Provo territory, where no hand dared to reach out and help. A prison officer had been murdered when his car stopped at these traffic lights, so it didn't matter to me if the lights were for or against me, I charged on through them. The roundabout at Carlisle Circus was the penultimate tricky part, then the gaol was reached.

I would do a 180-degree sweep and stop by the small gate at the front of the gaol; Roddy would get out and duck in through the door. Looking in all directions, I would pour on the coals until I was out of the killing zone, away from the high-rise where the tricolour flew, past St Patrick's Chapel, where my uncles were baptised, and then down into Royal Avenue and safety. Later, I would go over the route again to pick Roddy up.

When three months had passed without any word from the Belfast publisher about the manuscript I had sent them, I rang to enquire about it. 'I left a book with you,' I said, giving my name to the young lady who answered. 'It was about a sea battle.'

'It was about more than a sea battle. It was a marvellous social document.' (Mercy on all here!) 'We've got several other books and we want to publish them together shortly.'

'In what back?'

'In hardback.'

'Oh, right.'

All the stories, all the reflections, all the smiles and tears that I'd brought back to life over twenty years after the war had ended were to be made available to the public to read or not, to like or dislike. I was, as we say, up for cockshots. But I'd been there before, albeit within the confines of my work and my immediate acquaintances. Now I was to be judged by a hell of a bigger constituency.

There was more: how would my extended family react to the book? They had been uneasy for some time because of my trade-union activities. It was an area where Catholic names seemed to outnumber Protestant ones in the papers, and my name had appeared, linked to overtly celtic company. But this was minor compared to their anticipated reaction to the revelation of Mother's mixed background. I expected reaction from my brothers to beam outwards in concentric circles. It wouldn't be mentioned to me, that was their way, but it would not please them one bit. Since they weren't writers, they wouldn't appreciate the point that the cross-tribal thing makes for strong literature. And then there were the revelations about the pawnshop and the tick man. Pride would be wounded. This was 1977, long before it became the fashion for memoirs to begin with horror stories of neglect and abuse within the family and such stuff as dollars are made of. I never knew abuse. Our house was clean, we ate well on dip bread and bacon ends, on champ and ling, and the pillowcase full of Saturday's bread and buns on a Monday morning. Mother and Dad were darlings and dotes, they loved us and they loved each other, and we loved them, down where the dirt Protestants lived. I hoped that this would come through.

When the book was published it had a nice reception in the North and in the Republic. The *Irish Times* review by the late Eileen O'Brien made me smile. 'Mr McAughtry writes as well as the Belfast people talk, and that is very well indeed,' she wrote. 'It's just a pity that he hadn't stayed in Ireland, instead of going to the war.'

Eileen O'Brien was a strong nationalist, a lovely lady, and a fine parliamentary reporter. I came to know and respect her in the years to come. Her take on the Second World War was an Irish kind of a take, and I'm glad that she was the one to introduce me to the Irish way of thinking about it, because it made it easy for me to understand some of the spikier nationalists who were to raise the subject with me later. In any case, for many years now I have sat down to bimonthly lunches with Irish aircrew, many of whom flew in the war. We are all Irish together, and we have other things to talk about.

I was invited by the BBC in Belfast to talk about the book. It was my first broadcast and I was in a right state the night before. Even though I was well used to addressing audiences big or small, I had never been inside a broadcasting studio in my life and it worried me. I slept badly, was up out of bed far too early, and ended up in a downtown all-night café an hour and a half before the appointed time, eating an Ulster fry, drinking tea out of a thick mug, and yarning with a couple of dock labourers.

I was shown to a seat in the foyer of the BBC lobby and was beginning to think that the presenter had slept in, when he appeared about ten minutes before the pro-gramme was due to start. He was George Hamilton, who was to become one of the best sports commentators in

Ireland working for RTE. George introduced me to the other guest on the show, an academic gentleman who had written a book about Irish castles, and we were brought to the studio. By this time I was in a highly nervous state. What made matters worse was that George started with the other fellow. And away this other guest went, cool as a cucumber, and interesting with it: on top of his subject. The show was to last fifty minutes; I kept worrying that I would forget the details of the book. What a cock-up it would be if I forgot the names of any of the ships, or couldn't remember the names of the principals concerned. The clock was showing twenty minutes and I was worked up to the nines, when, during a three-second pause in his delivery, I heard my voice talking to the other guest. It was as if I was listening to someone else. 'I notice,' says I, 'that you haven't mentioned Carrickfergus Castle so far.'

The other man shook his head. 'My book's about Irish castles,' he said. 'Carrickfergus Castle's Norman.'

'It's a pity,' said the alien controlling me from Mars, 'because my Uncle Alec was locked up in Carrickfergus Castle. You hear tell of Essex, and Sorley Boy McDonnell, and even Francis Drake being in or about Carrickfergus, but nobody ever mentions my Uncle Alec.'

I then found, to my growing pleasure, that my nerves had retreated into the wings. I was in great nick. I used to interrupt serious conversations all the time, in this way, over drinks with senior civil servants and group captains in the RAF and earnest trade unionists. It was part mischief and part entertainment. George Hamilton was making signals to the producer, and the people behind the glass were pressing their faces against it.

'He was in the First World War, my Uncle Alec,' I went on. 'Before he left to go to France, his father, who was a committed communist, said to him, "Alec," he said, "don't be shooting the German privates, they're ordinary working men like us, but if you see any German officers, shoot them all right,"' and off I went and told the true tale of my Uncle Alec, who got drunk and overstayed his leave, fought the redcaps who had arrested him, and ended up in Carrickfergus Castle, which was a military prison in the First World War. When he had served his twenty-eight days' detention, he lined up for his pay, thinking that he would get twenty-eight shillings, which translated into eighty-four pints of stout, but all he got was twenty-eight pence, a penny a day being the going rate for military prisoners, so he wrecked the place and went back down to the dungeon.

'Nobody seems to know that,' I finished. 'See these history books? They're full of things about Essex and that lot. Not a word about my Uncle Alec. History's not what you know but who you know.'

In days to come I had a name for this tactic of interrupting a speech with a tale: I called it 'Rommel's right hook'. I was well into my fifties by that stage, and I hadn't the time to mess about. It was a bit like hooking the ball from a teammate, but with the other guy still having loads of time to do what he wanted; I didn't. I liked broadcasting, and I found myself using the old right hook a fair bit in the times to come. Leaving the studio, we met Gloria Hunniford coming in. She had heard the programme and asked me to send her three stories for her morning radio show. I submitted three soon after, but they were turned down by her producer. Later, I recorded the same three stories for RTÉ's radio programme *Sunday Miscellany*, and the station got a trayful of fan letters. Up the BBC's chuff.

Until the publication of my book I had known very little of the Northern Irish literary scene, my knowledge of writing being confined to journalism, but I certainly recognised Sam Hanna Bell when I called at the publishers one day and found him talking to the editor. I had long admired him for his wonderfully atmospheric novel *December Bride*. Through the Labour Party I knew that it was he who had first encouraged Sam Thompson to portray unionist bigotry in his play *Over the Bridge*, and I had greatly enjoyed Bell's pioneering folk material on BBC Radio Ulster, in the 60s and early 70s. When he had finished talking to the editor I was surprised to see that he was heading for me. He introduced himself: 'I'm starting up a literary miscellany in the *Ulster Tatler*, and I wondered if you might let me have a short story.'

As usual, when caught unawares, I dropped into smartass talk. 'Certainly,' I said. 'I'll knock something out for you and bung it in.'

He frowned, and Sam Hanna Bell's frown was ferocious. 'I don't want something that's knocked out and bunged in,' he said. 'I want a story that's written to the best of your ability.'

'Forgive me,' I replied. 'I'll be delighted to write for you and I hope you'll like it.'

Gone went the piercing stare, replaced instead with a warm smile. 'I'm sure it'll be excellent.'

The story appeared in the *Ulster Tatler* shortly after our initial meeting, alongside a hilarious little tale by the comic novelist John Morrow. I became friendly with John, and, not long before publication, he and I were together one evening at a cinema showing of some sort, when Sam appeared behind us. 'I greatly enjoyed your stories,' he said, and delighted both of us by talking about our work in the way that only a professional can.

After that, Sam Hanna Bell and I used to meet at the Stormont Hotel each Tuesday morning, he having retired from the BBC. We talked book talk; he was the first of a good many reputable northern writers to fill the great gaps in my knowledge of literature at that time, and I was charmed by the way in which he and the other authors, including award-winning writers, accepted me into their company. Literary recognition did not imply rank, and that was to apply in the future, all the way to the Nobel Laureate Seamus Heaney. Sam Hanna Bell died in 1990. I had known him for thirteen years. Long afterwards, Tuesday mornings at ten used to make me pause, and shake my head.

Bernard MacLaverty's first collection of short stories, *Secrets*, was published a few days before my book. I had been invited to the launch. I had never been to one before and this one was supposed to take place in the old Georgian house near Queen's University, where the Queen's English Society met, but so many turned up that we were all moved across the road to one of the university lecture theatres.

I remember a flushed and excited Edna Longley, the energy source for many years behind the English Society and indeed many other literary activities in Northern Ireland, telling me as we rushed along that the only other time the old house had been crowded out was during a reading by John McGahern, the author of so many brilliant novels, short stories and plays set in the Irish west midlands.

I took my seat in the front row of the lecture theatre as Barney MacLaverty, completely at ease, talked to a packed and appreciative audience, and read his beautifully crafted stories. He had been a mature student at Queen's, the audience included many of his fellow students, and the whole enthusiastic air of the occasion led me to believe that all book launches generated this level of warmth. I was wondering how on earth I would manage mine, but, in the event, it wasn't necessary. What happened was that I was called to the publishers and handed six hardback copies of the book, but just to feel their newness and to see my name on the cover was reward enough.

In 1981, shortly after I joined the *Irish Times* as a columnist, I wrote in light-hearted mood about the MacLaverty reading, and confessed that I sometimes imagined myself as the central figure in a similar scenario, with the place packed to capacity and latecomers, including well-known writers, sitting on the wooden steps and standing along the walls, as I acknowledged the introduction and began to address the audience. Little did I know that it would really happen.

A good many months later the English Society placed an advertisement in the northern papers announcing that I would read at its headquarters. By then I had attended a good many of its meetings and I considered that I had the run of the thing worked out, so I brought with me a sheet of paper on which I had scribbled an outline for a novel that I had in mind. Going on past form I was expecting an audience of about twenty; we would have a cosy chat, I would float the notion of the story, and we would toss it around, drinking coffee out of cardboard cups. When I reached the old Victorian house I was surprised at the number of people arriving. 'Are you here for the English Society?' I asked one couple.

They nodded, eagerly. 'There's a reading by Mac-Laverty,' they said.

I looked around. My goodness, it was like the evening of Barney MacLaverty's do. The place was packed. I stood outside, seriously thinking of getting the hell out of it.

Another thought struck me: sweet God, maybe they thought that Michael McLaverty was the star of the show. That was even more unsettling, as he was the author of the classic *Call My Brother Back*, seven other novels, three collections of beautiful short stories. I was just about to piss off when Edna Longley appeared, all flustered and flushed. She spotted me and took my arm. 'Come on, Sam, we'll have to use the lecture theatre.' As I hurried along beside her I heard her say, 'This is only the third time we've had to do this, the others were Bernard MacLaverty and John McGahern.'

I shrugged as I rushed along. McGahern's prose is soft,

insinuating and hynotic, and his detail is so fine. I didn't know what the audience expected, but I knew what they were going to get: no wristy tricks, as John Hewitt described his own style. I took my seat in the front row, holding my one sheet of sweaty paper, and watched the room fill up to bursting point, just as I had described it in my fantasy piece in the newspaper. I was introduced by Siobhan Kilfeather, daughter of John, who had been so kind to me when my book was published. In her opening words she called me Sam, thank Christ. There had always been problems with my surname: drill sergeants used to make it sound as if they were clearing their throats; in the North the usual attempt by strangers comes out as McCagherty, and in the South people in the street can't handle it at all, they just call me Sam ... er. So everybody knew the score. They were getting me. She mentioned in particular a short story of mine, about which she was very generous, then she beckoned to me and I was there, behind the big desk. I had to borrow one of my books from the front row.

After a short reading the rest of my talk didn't have a lot to do with literature. I talked to the audience about my family, about privation, destitution and decency, about the day in the depressed 20s when my father's ship was laid up for the want of work, when Dad took a stroll over to see his sister, my Aunt Lily, who lived on the New Lodge Road. He was back home in fifteen minutes. 'I had just reached the door when I smelt bacon frying,' he explained to Mother, 'so I turned and came back without knocking.'

I said that it was because of this background that I understood many things about working-class society in Belfast. Some on our side said that Catholics gambled in the bookie's far more than Protestants and so they did, but not because they lacked moral fibre: it was because the betting shop jumps on to poverty, and because the notion of getting the equivalent of a week's labouring wage for a couple of bob outlay could only seem reasonable to those who are unemployed week in, week out. When I was a youngster in Tiger's Bay we had poverty equalling the worst of that suffered by Catholics; we had no uncles, fathers, brothers in regular jobs to speak for us, no Freemasons, and, what a surprise, we were gamblers and heavy drinkers. And some of our men drank or gambled their dole money. Our homes weren't little palaces, like those of the Protestants on the Newtownards Road, stable families who lived stable lives. They knew that they could plan out their lives from Friday to Friday, while our men waited their turn for a day's work at the docks, or ploughed the ocean shovelling coal into furnaces, or dug the streets, or sat at coke fires taking sulphur into their lungs as nightwatchmen on outdoor relief work, and they were the ones who got work at all. The Catholic men who spent half the day with their backsides against the bookie's wall along North Queen Street wouldn't have had to look far to see us doing the same.

Why wouldn't I understand how Catholics felt? Hadn't I seen my own Uncle Thomas burnt out? But along with all of these things I knew, for I lived with it, the fear that Protestants felt at what might become of them in a Catholic all-Ireland. With southern independence, enough Protestants had been burnt out of the South to justify their fears. But this sort of material can't be delivered effectively if it isn't softened every now and again with humour, and I didn't neglect that side of things. The talk was well received and I drove home that evening shaking my head with disbelief.

The next morning at ten o'clock saw me sitting stride-legged across a chair, yarning with the chimney sweep about the state of the planet. He was good company, liberal-minded and well up with the political situation. We fell silent and listened to the ten o'clock news bulletin on the radio: it was the usual mix of republican mayhem and loyalist retaliation. It was followed by *Thought for Today*. The speaker was a priest. I started to talk to the sweep again when suddenly I heard my name mentioned on the air. 'I had prepared a script for this morning's talk,' the priest was saying, 'but I'm not going to use it. Last night I went to Queen's University to hear Sam McAughtry...' That's all I remember. It was an encomium to my outlook on life. As I cleared my throat and suddenly found a spot on the window pane to be fascinated with, the chimney sweep said, 'That was about you?' I nodded. 'Christ,' he said, 'I don't know what set that off, but I wouldn't walk up or down the Shankill for a while, if I were you.'

'*Ars longa, vita brevis*, as we say in Tiger's Bay,' I said.

It was in 1978 that I was delighted once again to meet up with Paddy Devlin. We had been members of the old Northern Ireland Labour Party, before it was melted down in the 1969 sectarian cauldron. A founder member of the Social Democratic Labour Party, Paddy had recently been expelled from the party because of disagreement with its policies and image. In his award-winning autobiography, *Straight Left*, he wrote:

On many occasions, when SDLP spokesmen took part in radio or TV programmes, they allowed the party to be described as a Catholic party. I complained about this, and challenged it in letters to the newspapers: only one other member, Denis Haughey, ever wrote in support ... It seemed to me that party strategy was solely directed towards consolidating the Catholic vote. I had left all that behind, apart from the period when the Catholic population in Belfast was under attack. I had been drawn into that unwillingly and I was determined not to be drawn into it again.

Devlin tried to form a labour party in 1980, but this attempt foundered, as have all other attempts to introduce normal left/right politics to the North's sectarian broth. He had always been interested in writing, and had self-published a book on the fall of the Sunningdale government in 1974. In that government, Devlin proved to be the only minister to gain cross-community support, even popularity, for the way in which he safeguarded the payment of social security benefits despite the efforts of those involved in the putsch to close Northern Ireland down completely.

From then until his death Paddy Devlin and I became very close. He wrote a play on dockland trade unionism which was staged at the Arts Theatre in Belfast; and he adapted Sam Thompson's celebrated exposé of loyalist sectarianism in the shipyard in the play *Over the Bridge*, which opened in the same theatre. Paddy also aired his trenchant views as a journalist and broadcaster and in his final years, in cooperation with Chris Ryder, the political author and journalist, there began the arrangement of his papers and the research that was to result in the excellent autobiography *Straight Left*.

In the last few months left to him he was honoured with

doctorates from both Northern Ireland universities, and earned a CBE for his work for peace. As to the latter, if he'd been at himself at all, I believe that he'd have declined the award graciously. He shared my own views as to the political lumber that the acceptance of such awards brings in a place so starved of the objective viewpoint. I will always be proud of the fact that Paddy Devlin and I worked so closely together for six years, countering the most politically illogical of all the IRA's activities – the bombing campaign against the Belfast to Dublin rail link. We launched the Peace Train Organisation (of which more later), and I was its chairman. For six years Paddy and I became a political twosome. He loved all sports, was a fine swimmer, soccer and Gaelic football player, and supported amateur and professional boxing enthusiastically. We were both members of the Northern Ireland Council of the British Boxing Board of Control, and in his declining months I would be his guide, for he was almost totally blind, and I would sit by him, describing the fight action. Walking through the welcoming crowds at the Ulster Hall or the King's Hall, he used to hold on firmly to my arm. The irony of it never escaped me: Paddy, who had done so much, relying on me. It was an honour to be so close to him.

To get back to the narrative, one of the nicest surprises of my life came when I first went down to Dublin to meet the folks at *Sunday Miscellany*. It was late 1978 and, during a broadcast of mine from the Belfast studio of RTÉ, Gerry McCann had phoned the show's producer, Maxwell Sweeney, and the next thing I knew I had received an invitation to come down and record some scripts in Montrose. A few months earlier I had gone down with some pals to see Down play football at Croke Park, and I had kept the business card of the bed and breakfast where we stayed, which happened to be in the Fairview area, on the north side, so that's where I booked in. This should give you some idea of how little I knew about Dublin. I needed a taxi to reach Montrose, so, when the driver let the clutch in, I said, 'I want to go to the radio part of RTÉ, not the TV part.' A man not too far from my own age, he gave me a sideways glance. 'You wouldn't be the fella that tells the stories on a Sunday mornin', would ye?'

For some reason I had never actually linked, to any great degree, the connection between broadcaster and listener. To me the audience was made up of the producer and the sound engineer. If they were happy I was happy. Without thinking about it, I had found the easiest road into relaxed broadcasting. 'I am indeed,' I said, all pleased. 'Did you hear me, then?' Yes, he had, and furthermore, he said he identified with me. It sounded a bit like Alcoholics Anonymous, but it was nice.

I was also surprised that the girl on reception at RTÉ knew me the moment I opened my mouth. I was introduced to Maxwell Sweeney and Ronnie Walsh, the man with the lovely, warm voice who presented the programme. After I had recorded the stories, the three of us went to the Royal Hibernian hotel for lunch. When it was my turn to order I'd only uttered a couple of words when the waiter stopped writing. 'Are you the gentleman who ...?' Maxwell and Ronnie laughed heartily at the expression on my face. The same thing happened in the bar later, when I ordered drinks. The barman told me he was disappointed to find that I didn't touch the drink, given all the stories of mine that were based in Dempsey's Bar. I was to meet this disappointment a hundred times in the future: a great many lovely, sociable people, including, once, Cardinal Tomás Ó Fiaich, looking forward to a drink in my company, were shaken when I ordered a mineral. It's a hell of a turn-off and it takes a good line in subsequent conversation on my part to settle the company down, but I was a good trier in this area.

When I got back to the digs the landlady rushed to make me a cup of tea. As I was drinking it in the lounge, she stopped by the door. 'Excuse me,' she said, 'but one of the guests says that you're Sam McCaffley – would he be right?' Oh, brother, I said to myself, but this is one hell of an improvement on the seat in the park. It was like being raised from the dead.

In 1980, while I was still working in the civil service, and had published a couple of books of short stories, Frank Delaney, who had been the BBC Northern Ireland's news correspondent in the Republic – probably the best ever, with a wonderful delivery – crossed over to the magazine department of Radio Ulster with a one-hour programme going out on Monday mornings. From the start he asked me to join him and I accepted with particular pleasure, while the BBC seemed mildly puzzled at his choice. This is where my speaking voice comes into the plot. I don't believe that in those early days the former teachers who seemed to run every sector of the Belfast station were happy with my delivery. It was probably for this class-conscious reason that they rejected the three stories that had made me well known in the Republic. Nearly every local presenter at that time made some kind of vowel-curtsy towards the Home Counties when they spoke on air. One or two of them actually sounded 100 per cent English. When I asked one of them why he did it, he replied that it was because he used to be an actor. I suppose the reason why I don't talk like that is because I wasn't an actor.

My voice raised the odd patronising smile among the more prissy producers. It used to amuse me. For ten years, as an air traffic controller in the RAF, I had worked with pilots from God knows how many countries, over carrier waves that sounded like broadcasts from Mars, and not a single flier seemed to share the BBC's problem with my delivery. Twenty-five years later things have changed, honest voices abound, but I still hear the odd Ormeau Avenue announcer who doesn't seem to know whether he or she comes from Belfast or Bletchley. Anyway, I wrote five-minute stories to introduce Frank Delaney's topic of the day.

It was interesting to observe how Delaney changed in those months from being a well-prepared chat-show host to the role of literary man. The BBC asked him to take over an ailing book programme on the UK network and he proceeded to give the show a shine that earned him a national award. Today he is a writer of stature and a sought-after judge of prestigious literary competitions. I have always had an affection for him because he insisted on having me on his programme on the first step of his own literary journey. On one of the shows a lady academic, listening to stories of the streets, described me as a 'primitive', a patronising visual arts term. Frank frowned, but I knew what she meant. I only wish that I had turned out to be a primitive in a smock instead of a writer hunched over a computer. Visual art is more lasting. I would far sooner be a good painter, and that's a fact, but that's life. I know my place in the league. I'm a compulsive writer, and I'm stuck with it. Some jerk might even have called John Osborne a primitive after the first showing of *Look Back in Anger*, who knows?

had a phone call one Saturday morning in 1980. It was from a lady who said that she was a researcher for the *Late Late Show*, her name was Pan Collins, and could I meet her at the Europa hotel? I had heard of this show, but since I couldn't receive RTÉ television because of the mountains of Mourne, I had rarely given it much thought. When I met Pan Collins over coffee she seemed surprised at my lack of knowledge of Gay Byrne and all who sailed with him. She was carrying a little book of my *Sunday Miscellany* broadcasts, not long published. She went through them, story by story, with a thoroughness that at first impressed me and then made me shift around in my seat with impatience. The lady made no apology for it: she wanted to know the background to the stories and she seemed to give a little nod of approval when I added a bit of extra humour to the telling.

The process was taking so long that I lied to Miss Collins and told her that I had to take my daily constitutional along the seafront at Donaghadee. In fact, this was to be the only time in my life that I took a midday constitutional anywhere. But, to my dismay, she asked if she could join me. So I put her into my car, and we drove to breezy Donaghadee. It was actually the first bloody time I'd gone to this quiet, pleasant seaside town since the kids were small. As we walked along the jetty, and up beside the lighthouse that was once given a coat of paint by Brendan Behan, I was questioned relentlessly not only about my own background, but about what I knew and thought of Dublin in particular and the Republic in general, which wasn't much.

When we left Donaghadee and Pan asked me to come into the Europa for more coffee I was driven to ask what the hell kind of a programme the *Late Late Show* was. 'Am I going to be psycho-analysed or something?' I wanted to know. By this time I knew so much about myself that I had had me up to the eyes. It reminded me of the clinic, and its analysis sessions. I said goodbye to the lady. Then I forgot all about the whole shebang and got on with things more immediate.

It was over a week later that Pan Collins called. 'I hope you'll accept our invitation to come on the show as a guest,' she said.

'Is this fella going to pull and haul at me the way you did?' I asked.

She laughed heartily. 'It's just that there's a panel of two who sit near Gay and come in with their views on the topic of the evening. I was trying you out for a regular slot, but you're too innocent of our wily ways. I'm sure you'll enjoy the show.'

The evening of the show represented one of the high-lights of the new life that I had been given. I remember every single detail of it. RTÉ put me up in the Montrose hotel on the evening of the show. I had a few hours to kill, so I took a taxi to the centre of Dublin, looking in shop windows, listening to the voices of the Dubliners as they passed. I went into a pub at the corner of D'Olier Street and fell into a conversation with a lady with soft eyes. 'Are you from the North for a break?' she asked. I told her yes. 'You'll be all right here,' she said. 'There's nobody'll touch you down here.' There was nobody touching me up there, either, but I didn't want to send her flying by revealing that I was a black Protestant.

Back in the Montrose hotel I had a nice snack, the car came for me, and I was taken to the television centre to meet the other guests: Robert Kee, the historian, and Clive Dunn, the wonderful Corporal Jones, from the classic television show *Dad's Army*. Kee had just published a history of Ireland and was presenting a television series running concurrently. He was a most agreeable man, a clear speaker, a former RAF pilot who had been shot down early in the war and had written a much-praised book on his experiences in captivity.

I was to open the show. In the years to come I was to grow accustomed to this. Presenters by the dozen would assume that I had no nerves. It must have been something about my manner. In fact, in the wings, I was as nervous as any other performer, but I was lucky in knowing that the nerves would go as soon as I got the first words out on the set. The girl who escorted me to the entry point behind the scenes was amazed to learn that I had never actually seen the show. 'What goes on?' I wanted to know. I had it in my head that I might have to take part in some kind of parlour game.

She shook her head. 'It's too late to tell you now; you're on in seconds. Break a leg. Just go over, take your applause, shake hands with Gay and sit down.'

That's how I came to appear on the first of dozens of live television shows as a guest. I could hear Gay working the audience, then I heard him introduce me, there was a burst of applause, and I walked out into the warm studio lights, saw Gay, shook hands and sat down. I looked the audience over, and was surprised at the numbers. There was a lovely, anticipatory feeling about the place.

The first feeling that came to me had nothing to do with the show. It was the realisation that these people belonged to a different society from the one in which I had been reared. This was their television station, in their capital city. It was like being outside my Ireland, in another country. They had their own radio and TV programmes, they had their own parliament, their own sporting idols, even their own sport, one that even reflected their own politics. For them there had been no war, no Luftwaffe obliteration of city centres. Hitler had even compensated them for an accidental bombing by a Luftwaffe plane. In the Troubles they'd had a loyalist bombing outrage, but no wholesale bombing of businesses or murders of politicians, no tit-for-tat killings by loyalist assassins. None of their political parties had ever wanted to tie up the swings in public parks on a Sunday. They had a proper Labour Party. The overriding feeling that came across from the smiling audience was of a society at ease with itself and with its institutions of state, but the Irishness that I had always felt within myself was not like theirs at all. I didn't think that they saw an Irishman when they saw me. They were welcoming me to their relaxed society as an interesting individual from outside their Ireland. It was like somebody from war-blattered Paris visiting French-speaking Quebec.

The chat, when it started, was pure pleasure. Pan Collins had done a lovely job. Without a note in sight, Gay pressed the buttons, became my buddy for ten minutes, listened to me rattle off two or three of the reminiscences from my book, then he rose and went over to the audience, where hands were going up all over the place.

The questions were serious and political, which suited me. The subject of separate education for Catholics was raised by one lady, who objected to it and said that she was going to send her child to a mixed-religion school. Others were curious to know about my growing up in a loyalist area, and I was happy to talk about the per-ceptions of my friends and neighbours, and the fact that we had shared the economic deprivation of the 1920s and early 1930s with Dublin.

I made clear my Irishness, and it seemed to strike some as a bit odd, even eccentric, coming from someone who had fought in the Second World War, and was clearly happy to live under the UK system of government. I pointed out that my parents had just come out of an all-Ireland state, albeit under the Crown, so their heroes and our childhood heroes were the likes of Jimmy O'Dea, Harry O'Donovan and John McCormack, and that as a family we listened to Dublin Athlone and Cork, as the RTÉ station was known then. Of course, the Irishness was all but driven out of the next generation, when Stormont began to lean on Catholics, and the South claimed the North, without altering any of its institutions or mindsets in advance to accommodate us. I think I mentioned that last bit, although I've said it so many times since the show that I could be wrong. As to the contributions of the two star guests, it was a privilege to share the same set with them. We were all three ex-servicemen, and there is a special bond between wartime comrades.

Next morning, when I came down to breakfast in the Montrose hotel, fellow guests were looking at me, and whispering and smiling. 'Welcome to Dublin,' one man said.

'It's all very nice,' I told him, and it was all that, all right.

Pan Collins wrote a book about the *Late Late Show*, published in 1981 by Ward River Press. In her preface she described herself as, '. . . a fat, sixty-five-year-old widow, in no way pass remarkable, indeed, rather chunky . . .' but I remember her as lovely and warm and kindly. I have her book, and its message: 'For dear Sam McAughtry, a star of the *Late Late Show*'s 19th season – With affection.' To this I might add that, if prayers can help her rest in peace, mine have been added to the great host of others that followed her passing.

Meanwhile, on my next visit to Dublin, I was asked by a man in the street to pose for a picture under the flag of the Republic. He was tickled pink. 'It's great that you don't mind,' he said. This was to happen to me a good many times in different towns, and once on Inish More. It is as much the fault of unionists as of citizens of the Republic that the latter should assume the northern Protestant to be some kind of Hottentot.

While I was still in the civil service the *Irish Times* sent Eugene McEldowney to Belfast to profile me. Eugene, at that time the paper's industrial correspondent, came from Ardoyne, an area in Belfast as fiercely republican as Tiger's Bay was loyalist. Interestingly, a great-uncle of Eugene's, Paddy McEldowney, was a highly respected publican whose business was at the foot of Cosgrave Street, where I was born, so, once this was established, the interview was off to a flying start. It was when it appeared in the *Irish Times* that I had my first lesson in how the Republic saw Belfast's working-class Protestants. 'On meeting Sam McAughtry, one is surprised,' Eugene's piece began. 'He is a tall man, with a mop of white hair.'

That's instead of being comically small, with brilliant-ined hair, wearing the six-pointed Ulster star tie, with a flute-band swagger, and supporting Linfield and Glasgow Rangers. Tall, and with a mop of white hair – goodness, I might almost be mistaken for a normal person, maybe even a Catholic. But Eugene was writing for a southern readership: he had more sense than to typecast Protestants. Later, when I came to write for the paper, Eugene told me that there were times when the views in my column made him swear, but it was nice to be told this in such a direct and healthy way, not that it changed my perception of things. Here at home, my only close buddy for over fifty years is a firm nationalist, and he remains as solid a friend today, after a hundred arguments, as when we first met, and got drunk together, and made each other laugh, in 1948.

In mid-1981 I left the civil service on a Friday and started work for the *Irish Times* the following Monday. I didn't know until later that the paper was fighting its way out of a crisis, the circulation having fallen drastically. Douglas Gageby had been brought back from retirement to take over the editorship as a matter of urgency, and I was part of the recovery plan, together with a brilliant team of editors, journalists and analysts. Conor O'Clery was on the news desk and heavy hitters like Conor Cruise O'Brien and John Healy were here too, with Donal Foley, Mary Mahon, Claud Cockburn and Maeve Binchy lighting up the features pages.

There was an air of crisis in the building: I remember Donal Foley and Bruce Williamson telling me about other Dublin papers that had folded. 'It happens so suddenly,'

Bruce said. 'You turn up for work and are told to go back home.' Meanwhile, Kevin Myers, a man who could have jacked up the circulation significantly, was held back by Douglas, who didn't fancy his work, but brilliant Kevin's day would come when Douglas retired.

In broadcasts from the BBC and RTÉ I was edging away from the picaresque sort of material that had helped to bring me notice. I was offering contributions that had a more universal appeal, and wise Donal Foley spotted it. 'Don't forget,' he said, 'you are our remembrancer. Don't leave that behind.'

After the strict rank structure and the prissy attitude in the civil service, it was good to be in journalism, where the emphasis was on producing the work within the set time, and after that whatever you're having yourself. I was even given the honour of starting the presses. In my first week there I was invited by Conor O'Clery to a party in his Dublin home. Dick Walsh was one of the guests, and he told the following story. It was somebody's birthday, the bar in Fleet Street was packed with *Irish Times* workers, and Maeve Binchy arrived late, ending up at the door, pressed against a man who was known to be a master groper. He leered at Maeve and his hand began to travel, but before it reached the point of no return Maeve grabbed it and clapped it over her generous bosom. 'Right,' she said, 'let's get it over and done with, and then let me through.' Apparently a complete cure was effected.

Nineteen eighty-one was the year that the IRA hunger strikes claimed ten lives. RTÉ had asked me to present a programme showing life on both sides in north Belfast. I went to a Provo-run club on the Oldpark Road on the afternoon of the filming and got the agreement of the club secretary to come in that evening and meet some of the customers. I next spoke to Andy Tyrie, the then leader of the UDA, and got his permission to visit a loyalist-run club on the Shore Road.

I met the crew at the railway station and told Brian Black, the producer, that all was set for a good, lively survey of north Belfast, where there had been more casualties and suffering than in any other part of the North. In the early evening we filmed some local background, then, at around seven o'clock, we went to the Oldpark Road club. As the crew were getting their gear together, I spoke to my star guest, a perky little pensioner whom I'd known for most of my life. I was sitting, laughing at one of his recollections, when we were interrupted by a burly, low-set man, about thirty years old, with his face sculpted into that same sour, venomous expression I'd first seen on the faces of loyalist gunmen who had come to order a Catholic barman out of the pub in the Protestant part of east Belfast, where I used to live in 1969, when the Troubles started properly.

'Who are you and what are you doing here?'

'Oh, right, hello. Well, I'm from RTÉ and we're making a film about north Belfast, particularly the role of clubs like this one, in providing some sort of social life for the people. I've squared it with the manager.'

'What's the object?'

He was drilling holes with his eyes into mine, and I wasn't one to go along with that. I tried to cover my annoyance. 'These clubs fill a social need, linked to the times. They're not just drinking clubs. There are people here to talk their problems out and others to listen. They're not like pubs.'

'It's political.'

'How the hell can you make that out to be political?'

Brian and the crew were already packing their stuff. By now I was taking this guy on, look for look. He would be high in the local IRA command: the days were still to come when such people would wear expensive suits and strut before the cameras. I was seeing, for the first time in my life, one of the bogeymen from tales told to me through all of my growing-up days. There was contempt, even hatred, in his eyes, and, for the few seconds involved, he was getting it back. I was going to have to go, but I didn't like it, or him, and I was hoping it showed.

'Whereabouts do you come from, anyway?' He was registering my mood. He knew the look. He wasn't seeing a television presenter now: he was looking at the loyalist side of Duncairn Gardens.

'They all know him here,' the old pensioner piped up, 'they would all know him here.'

'Get to fuck out of it and do it now.'

Later, Paddy Devlin drew in his breath when I repeated the exchanges. 'Some of these guys are doped up to the eyeballs,' he said. 'When they say go, you go quietly.'

Outside the club, the Oldpark Road was in total darkness. The Provos had snuffed out every light. The empty road, the black dark, the silence, and the dread was almost palpable. 'The hunger strike starts tomorrow,' Brian said. That's when I knew that this hunger strike would bring with it a hell of a lot more violence in the community than an earlier one that had petered out, but that was how every aspect of the conflict was going.

As we waited while the gear was loaded, a helicopter blattered overhead. Suddenly its blue-white beam found us. We were standing together, the sound engineer holding his stand in a rifleman's order arms position. The blinding beam held us for a few seconds, then it blinked out. I'll say this for the young RTÉ crew, they were game. We climbed into the car and went down to the Shore Road; the others sat in the car while I went in to see the UDA committee. They were geniality itself.

'The crew are from Dublin,' I explained.

'That's no problem,' they said. 'Sure Andy Tyrie said to look after you.'

They gave us beer and sandwiches and tea, they told funny stories, and the old Tiger's Bay folk talked to us about the Protestant area from where they'd been moved to the cold, bleak Shore Road, by the side of Belfast Lough. The heating in their new houses was inadequate, their community had been scattered to the edges of the city by what they considered to be a distinct plan to reduce friction at flashpoint areas by reducing the Protestant numbers in each location. In later years, well into the ceasefire, the reduced quotas of Protestants at peace lines were to be heavily outnumbered by nationalists. Sinn Féin needling replaced the Orange triumphalism of earlier years, but on that evening in 1981 we were relieved just to be able to get a programme of sorts out of what had at one time looked like a complete failure to carry out our assignment.

Meanwhile, Bobby Sands and nine others were preparing to die, while in the background the IRA and the UDA were planning deaths of a more immediate kind.

*

The best colour writer I have ever enjoyed, in any newspaper, was Maeve Binchy, who had not yet become the bestselling novelist she is today, although she had written some lovely short stories and plays. My favourite example of her style of self-deprecating humour came in her description of a journey she made in a helicopter with Charles Haughey to one of the islands, during one of several general election campaigns in the early 1980s. 'As the party stepped down from the helicopter and made their way towards the group of islanders waiting to welcome us,' Maeve wrote, 'I was thinking to myself, I suppose these people will be wondering who is the mysterious lady accompanying Charles Haughey...'

Haughey himself was very friendly towards me. He would pick me out of crowds of journalists for a friendly word, or a leg-pull. I suppose it was because he shared the widespread view in the Republic that I was a live, bushy-tailed unionist, not afraid to come down and mix with republicans and act the Irishman.

He was excellent company. I once shared a table with him at an annual dinner of International PEN, the world association of writers, and thoroughly enjoyed the evening. When the speeches began one of the guests congratulated him on having introduced tax-free status for creative artists; when it was my turn I mentioned that Mr Haughey wasn't all that well known where I came from, because, before leaving Comber, I had told my newsagent that I was going to Dublin to meet Charlie Haughey.

'Would he be anything to Tommy Haughey from Killinchy, who used to work in the shipyard?' the paper man asked.

When the time came for Charlie to reply, he began by thanking the first speaker for his kind comments on the tax-free concession. 'He was too generous, altogether,' the former Taoiseach went on, 'I didn't recognise myself. For a minute there I thought he was talking about Tommy Haughey from Killinchy, who used to work in the shipyard.'

In his book *Recollections of a Writer by Accident*, published in 2003, J. Anthony Gaughan remembers Haughey that evening as being '. . . taciturn and seemingly in a troubled state of mind,' but in my company he was most entertaining. Maybe I helped lift his troubles for a bit.

During a general election in 1982 I was one of the press party accompanying Haughey on his rounds in Dun Laoghaire. As he left the local hospital, with fawning Fianna Fail colleagues on either side of him, he beckoned me to join him, and, with one arm around my shoulder, smiled for the cameras and set off on a tour of the town. In between glad-handing the locals he spoke to me of his concern for both sides in the northern conflict. 'The unionists would be surprised at the generosity we would show them,' he said. Later, he was to use the expression in a major speech.

I mentioned to him something about IRA men and women running the streets in the Republic openly. 'I've met them, heard them boast about it,' I said.

'Ah, sure, the half of them are on the run from their wives,' Charlie said. 'They make up that stuff about the IRA: it makes big fellas out of them.'

Seconds later, as we were walking past a shop on the main street, Charlie saw a man at the doorway; he waved and said hello. 'You can stuff your hello,' the man said, in a low voice. 'I wouldn't vote for you if you were to give me a million. You're a bloody crook, and all belonging to you.'

Charlie Haughey smiled, as if he'd just been paid the highest of compliments. He put his face close to my ear. 'And up yours too,' he whispered. I burst out laughing, and so did he, and the media out on the road, walking alongside, took quick photos. They were thinking, I suppose, that the pair of us were getting along famously. Which, indeed, we were.

I know my recollections of Charlie Haughey should be coloured by the disgrace which followed revelations at a corruption tribunal in the mid-1990s, and his consequent retreat in some haste from public life, but, having met him a good many times in the last half of the 1980s, I still admit to a liking for the man. Unfortunately, the first evidence of his involvement in scandal coincided with an invitation for him to come on to RTÉ and chat to me. He could not possibly accept. It's a pity: outside of politics we were an interesting mix, the pair of us.

In 1983, during one of my lunches with Douglas Gageby, I happened to mention that my father was buried in Cuba, and that, although I had had lots of seagoing relatives and friends in the years after he died in 1951, none had ever called at a Cuban port, so I had no idea where he was buried, or what his resting place looked like. I had, in the early 1970s, written to the British Embassy in Havana asking for the necessary details, but, after long months, I received a letter telling me that the appropriate records were not available. I had assumed that they had been lost in the revolution of 1959, when Fidel Castro had overthrown the Batista regime. It had seemed then as though the short trail had run out, and I had given up. It was a pity, I said to Douglas, because I had developed a liking for history through working on my first book. I told him how excited I had been, having gone to sources from the start, to find errors or gaps in the work of earlier writers who had dealt with the Battle of the Atlantic in the Second World War, and the attack on the *Jervis Bay* convoy in November 1940 in particular. All of this had heightened my need to know a great deal more about an important part of my own family history. I knew only sketchily the circumstances of my father's death, and it was a situation hard to accept.

Douglas the historian understood how I felt. He was also, for twenty-four hours a day, a man whose antenna was searching for good feature stories. 'Why don't you go to Havana for the *Irish Times*, write me a piece on how the working class there live, and go and look for your father's grave?' he suggested.

I was delighted. I rang the Cuban Embassy in London the very next day, explained the circumstances, asked for press accreditation, and made an early appointment. When I got there the public relations man, who looked like a black film star, was a bit doubtful. 'I've asked Havana to look into this,' he said, 'but I don't know...' He shook his head.

Hell roast this, I thought, I'm not going to be brought down at this fence as well.

'This isn't just a family enquiry,' I said. 'I work for the *Irish Times*, it's a paper read all over the world. This is a human interest story. If your people can bring me to my father's grave it will look good for Cuba. I am also instructed to bring back a story about the working class in Havana. I have trade union credentials in my own right, and I know what to look for in that area. Anyway,' I finished up, 'I want to meet the Olympic champion Teofilio Stevenson, the greatest heavyweight who ever lived, as well as the other things.'

I was putting on the Irish. The press officer smiled, offered me a Cuban cigar, arranged for coffee to be provided, and went to the phone. He spoke for about twenty minutes, then he came out and asked me if I had anything else to do in London for the next hour. I went to the Imperial War Museum in Kennington, and saw on display the 617 Squadron sergeants' mess meal list for the RAF aircrews who flew on the dams raid in 1943. There was a tick against the names of all who took the traditional bacon and egg meal before take-off, and the tick was crossed against those who returned to sit down to another of the same. Of 133 aircrew taking part, fifty-three did not return. The uncrossed ticks put me in a subdued mood as I sat on the bus taking me back to the Cuban Embassy.

My father had known nothing but seafaring. He was the son of a master mariner and had sailed on coasters from the age of thirteen. When he was fifteen, in 1897, his father was drowned in Liverpool Bay and Dad, as the only boy in a family of five, was sent across to identify the body and arrange for its return home. After completing the paperwork he signed on an oceangoing ship as a coal trimmer, and stayed at sea on various ships for the next three years. On the day he returned home his mother turned from the mantelpiece, saw him, and said, 'So it's you.' In all, he was at sea for fifty-six years. We saw him on average once every three months, for a four- or five-day stay.

He was an only son, with four lively sisters. His mother, my grandmother, lived with daughters all around her, over on the New Lodge Road, in Shandon Street. She was a formidable old lady, small, dressed all in black, and she was well read, very loyalist, and probably felt intellectually stranded, because her daughters were too busy rearing their families to worry about developments in the

Irish Free State, or the progress of the Spanish Civil War. As children we were ordered over to visit her when we had new clothes or new shoes. I think that Mother missed no opportunity to show Gramma that her son had married wisely.

In the first air raid of 1941 Gramma's house was levelled, but she was dug out, dusty, testy, and very much alive. She was brought to our house and Mother went to get the brandy. 'Lizzie,' Gramma called. 'Don't be putting any water into that brandy. I'm in no mood for water.'

My old dad came from tough stock.

My father was torpedoed in both wars, was three days in an open boat in the Denmark Strait in winter, in 1942, at sixty years of age. He kept on sailing the terrible North Atlantic run even after my brother Mart was lost at the start of the Second World War. Dad was five foot seven, weighed eight and a half stone, and he was typical of the merchant seamen whose losses in the second war were greater as a percentage than those of any of the uniformed forces. In his last years he was terrified at the prospect of ending up ashore as a pensioner, so the company averted their eyes while he falsified his age and stayed seafaring. He was sixty-nine when he died in agony from peritonitis, in the sickbay of a sugar company in a tiny Cuban port where his last ship docked to put him ashore. His captain left the money for him to come back home, but he never did. He had no savings when he died. The Inland Revenue got shirty about his posthumous tax debt and threatened distraint of goods, but they dropped the charges 'without prejudice' when I sent them the draft of an article I proposed to submit to the press if they seized so much as a cushion from our house. I wrote in the article that they were dishing out bloody medals to the uniformed forces for lesser contributions to the war effort, but the country was repaying him through distraint.

When I went back to the Cuban Embassy the press attaché said, 'I can give you the go-ahead. They haven't got all the details you need, but there's enough to make a visit worthwhile.'

In May 1983, excited as a scout going to summer camp, I boarded a Russian airliner at Shannon airport. I was squeezed into a seat occupied by a lady of about eighteen stone on the one side and a taciturn Russian man on the other. The aircraft had begun its journey in Moscow, the passengers had gone bonkers in the duty-free and the air inside the plane was a mixture of perfume and Paddy whiskey. Across the aisle from me a passenger had a copy of the *Sun* newspaper. He had discovered Page Three and he and the Cuban men in front and behind were laughing and talking like machine guns. When they caught my eye I laughed too, and for the next hour or so, through one of their number who spoke English, I was answering questions about Britain. They weren't much interested in Ireland. They wanted to know about industrial strikes, pickets and the level of wages; what could be bought with a week's pay, and the sort of style in which Mrs Thatcher and her cabinet lived. I was happy to inform them that Mr Dennis Thatcher and his son Mark were probably making a fortune at whatever they did, because of the address at the top of their stationery.

The Cubans around me were more lively and sociable

than the Russians and East Germans among the passengers, although the Russian stewardesses couldn't have
been more attentive. I was to learn later that there wasn't a
lot of socialising between the Russian engineers and
advisers and the Cubans; it was certainly evident on the
plane, but anyway, anticipation made the time pass
quickly for me.

We arrived at Havana and joined the circuit with the
steepest banking turn I have ever experienced in a
passenger aircraft. There was a huge queue at the passport
desk; the army man there was pure Hollywood Mexican,
studying each arrival against the passport photo, picking
his teeth, looking at checklists under the window, examin-
ing his nails: I was loving all of it, despite the time wasted.
'Why you here?' I was asked. Without Spanish there was
no way I was about to mention my primary quest, so I
said, 'Prensa,' and showed him my press card, plus my
brand-new Irish passport, and after a long phone call I was
waved past. However, the excitement and euphoria were
soon to be flattened when a woman sitting behind a desk
in the arrivals hall took a fistful of dollars from me to pay
for my stay in the Hotel Deauville. It left me almost
cleaned out. I had no credit card, and I had grown so used
to the *Irish Times* girl reserving accommodation for me that
I had assumed that it had been arranged here, in advance.
The hardship it was eventually to cause made me take out
not one but three credit cards, plus an EEC chequebook,
when I returned to Dublin.

For a chat merchant like myself it was a desolate feeling
to have no Spanish. The Cuban hotel staff were so friendly
and talkative that it was like physical pain to be unable to
reply. In some desperation I fastened on to a Canadian
airline pilot who made regular stopovers in Havana. His

view on Cuba was on the bilious side: 'These poor bastards get twelve ounces of meat every ten days, and they gotta take whatever kinda meat is offered.' He shook his head. 'They got nothin' to look forward to, nothin'. Take a look at those women behind the bar; they look pregnant, but they're just fat on starchy food to make up for lack of meat.'

Sure enough, the two young women concerned were carrying a little bit of condition, but I only nodded agreement because the Canadian was an English-speaking oasis in the Spanish desert. Actually, I wanted to like everything Cuban. There would forever be a close link between this island and my family.

The famed communist system worked behind the bar: one lady took my order, wrote it down and handed the note to a second lady, who prepared the drink and passed the note to a third lady, who ran the till. After the till rattled the drink reached the customer's hand. I was reminded of some communist friends back home who wanted Ireland to be run the same way, and I was speculating on how the typical Irish drinker's temperament would stand up to having to wait, on a crowded Saturday night, as his drink order went through this deliberate little dance routine before the Guinness actually hit the throat.

The Canadian pilot had plenty to say about this communist charade, as he put it, but I couldn't help remarking that to the natives it was better than working for the Mafia in an island-sized brothel.

'You're right enough about the Yank thing,' he conceded, 'but don't expect too much help in finding your father's grave. Hate to say it, but the Cubans work very slowly, when they work at all, and the seven days you've got won't be nearly enough to get them going.'

That night in bed I came over all thoughtful: a piece on the Havana working class on its own would maybe interest the readers, but the family thing was the beef in the sandwich. To the sound of a broken air-conditioner I popped a tab and flaked out.

Next morning at 8.30 I sat in the *ministerio*, looking around and thinking that it wasn't much like the Ministerio del Agriculture, Irlanda del Norte. The Cuban government had taken over an entire area where the upper classes had once lived: pleasant, comfortable houses, in wide, cool, quiet avenues, and the press office was located in one of these. A door opened and in walked a dusky young lady. 'I am Alba Holder,' she said, 'and I am here to look after you.'

'When you say looking after me, what do you mean, Alba Holder?'

'On Wednesday I am going to take you to see your father's grave.' She was smiling at my reaction. I did a little dance. 'You should have been a Cuban,' she said, when I finished by swinging her around.

With three days to wait I went out to meet the ordinary people of Havana. I talked to a group of young fellows who were erecting a rickety-looking wooden scaffolding outside an old building in the heart of the city. Tomaso spoke fair English, but his talking stopped and the eyeballs of the whole group popped out when a black girl of about seventeen walked past. She was wearing stiletto heels, very beautiful, slim, dressed in gingham, as though just out of a Hollywood musical. She smiled a nice, natural smile at the whistles and attention she was getting. When all motor impulses were back under control I said, 'About blacks in Cuba – are they equal in every way?'

All four workmen, born after the revolution, agreed that this was so. 'Oh, yes, I like to treat that one as equal,' Tomaso said, with shining eyes, then he had a conversation with his buddies. 'They say, sometimes when the woman is white and the man is black, we don't like it so much.' One of the squad added to Tomaso that he had followed his father in this way of thinking.

The one thing that every visitor to Cuba, right up to the present time, has had to admit about the Castro regime is that the government has certainly vastly improved the level of education of the people, whatever the other democratic shortcomings. The people whom I met, who grew up after the revolution, were bright and full of curiosity about the West's way of life. There was very little envy, except from the currency spivs who hung around the sea wall, and this was still so when I made a second visit for the BBC in the mid-1990s, but on that first visit I was an object of great interest to students, who seemed to be everywhere. Once, I was practically hauled into a coffee shop by a group of female students anxious to talk about British politics, including the use of women in TV advertising, and *Playboy*-type magazines. I told them that in Britain and Ireland women still lagged behind in pay and promotion; their mouths fell open when I recounted the trade union campaign in which I had taken part, in the 1960s, to abolish the practice of sacking women in the civil service and banking profession upon marriage. In other areas, I said, women's lives had been improved by way of laws to protect the interests of women in broken marriages or common-law relationships.

I met a bartender who had bridged the Batista and Castro years, and I encouraged him to talk about the time before the revolution. He spoke American-English in a deep, hoarse voice. I asked him to compare pay and conditions of work with the rates at present. 'Today, I get ninety pesos every fifteen days,' he said. 'In the old days I could have earned that in a couple of days in this bar.'

'Mostly tips, I suppose?' Tipping was not encouraged under the Castro regime.

'To shut my mouth, to open my mouth. Never for just working. The big tips were to keep the monkey business going.'

'What sort of monkey business?' I was soon sorry I'd asked. He told me about a Cuban girl keeping company with an American gangster. The man wanted her to go home with one of his pals, and the girl refused, and kept on refusing, until the other man gave up and walked away. The gangster then broke a bottle and blinded the girl with it. She was taxied to hospital and the bar staff all received hefty tips to keep mum.

'Today ninety pesos,' the bartender growled, 'but there's no more monkey business.'

I joined five old-timers, all men, who were sitting on the front step of their apartment block. They moved over to make room for me. I gathered that there was some talk about me in the neighbourhood, and they wanted to know all about me, so I told them through the ubiquitous one who spoke some American-English. They confirmed the Canadian's account of the meat rationing, but didn't seem in the least bit fazed about it. As ever, I kept regretting that I couldn't talk to them in my own way, throwing in my own embellishments, but they soon read the signals and we became quite chummy. I think it was evident to them that I had known rough grub times myself. I asked them if they earned enough to allow for a few drinks on a Saturday night and their glances said, 'We wish.' On the subject of the booze, my guidebook said that there wasn't much drunkenness on the island, but I told the old-timers that, in the course of a taxi ride the previous evening, some young Cuban men, obviously tanked, had jumped into the path of the taxi and back again, waving their fists at the driver and shouting what I took to be Cuban cursing, and the old ones laughed. 'Too much *ron* [rum]. Every night it's fight or cry.' Seemingly they were assumed to be students, so nothing in the world changes.

On the Tuesday I used the last of my travelling money to take a look at the nearest beach. I had been living on scrambled eggs and rough bread for breakfast, dinner and tea since arriving, and I had exactly enough to do me for scrambled eggs and rough bread up until the last day. The scrambled eggs were terrible. It couldn't have been a national dish. The taxi driver who had been carrying me for the previous couple of days was a philosopher. 'When you haven't got any more dollars,' he said, 'you haven't got any more taxi.' But he waited for the hour or so that I walked along the beach in my Marks & Spencer shirt, shorts and beach shoes, and my borrowed camera, a fine-quality Canon A1 with zoom lens.

The beach was wondrously beautiful – white, spotless sands stretched for miles, and it was, magically, almost empty. I couldn't believe that such a beautiful place should be so short of visitors (this was well before Cuba managed to put in place a kind of infrastructure for tourism). Almost the only people there were little groups of local boys and girls playing ball games. As soon as the girls spotted me I became something of a celebrity. My duty-free sunglasses and the camera were the main attraction. The girls came shyly over to me as the boys stood watching. One of the girls pointed to the camera and I asked her to pose with her three or four friends: they giggled all the time as I snapped them. They looked absolutely stunning, around seventeen; it was agony to be unable to talk to them, but I guessed that they were third-level students, and it was lovely for me to be white-haired and unthreatening and to have my smiles returned in the most natural way, while the boys stood watching.

'English?' they asked.

I shook my head. 'Irlanda.'

They looked blank.

I walked slowly for half a mile along the beach and each time I met a group of young ones. The girls came running over and after the second live shot I had to pretend that I was taking their photographs, for I would need the couple of rolls of film that I had for the burial place. Once, one of the boys asked to see the camera: he almost kissed it as he turned it over, examined the lens and the controls, and put it to his eye. All of this was done in reverent silence. A girl pointed to the sunglasses and I gave them to her. She put them on, but when I gestured to her to keep them she declined, gracefully. To them I was no Captain Cook. From old-age pensioners to teenage shop assistants, I have never seen the equal of the dignity shown by the people of Havana when I was there in 1983.

There was one question which needed answering, though: after four hundred years of Spanish influence, how did religion sit alongside communism? I had actually landed there on Good Friday, the most prayerful day of the Christian year. On Easter Sunday I went to 10 o'clock Mass at the 300-year-old cathedral of San Cristobal. Its two huge bells, cast in Spain in 1700, pealed out across San Ignacio Square and beyond, carrying to the docks, where the Russian freighter, the *Captain Potemko*, was unloading. There were about two hundred worshippers at the service, nearly all of them tourists from South America. Up in the high roof space birds fluttered and chuckled. The cathedral badly needed repairs. When the service ended I learned that the bishop didn't give press interviews, so I went across the square and spoke to local people outside their houses. They told me that they had no interest in the church and never attended. Later, I spoke to a senior member of the central committee of the communist party in Havana. 'We were never a religious people,' he told me. 'We lost all that under colonial rule. The bishops and the rulers were too close.' He added that church leaders were not consulted any more on education or moral matters.

Between the time of my second visit to Cuba ten years later and the end of the millennium Russian influence had ended there. After decades of economic siege by America, conditions on the island were difficult: there was much poverty and the people were suffering. But they suffered more when Batista ruled, the people were made servants to the Americans, and they were colonised for centuries before that. Castro's rule was tight and uncompromising and there was a civil rights shortfall which we in our society would not have tolerated, but it would seem that the great majority of Cubans wanted no change. He had given all of them the opportunity to read and write and paint and dance and make music and think to the limit of their abilities. He reversed half a millennium of servitude. That has to be conceded, even by the USA.

I went to meet Alba Holder and began the journey to my father's grave feeling indebted to the people of Havana. They had allowed me into their lives to a far greater extent than is set down here. Because of my shortage of cash I had spent hours just wandering the streets, stopping people and talking to them. Each one of them had been courteous and outgoing. Many were curious to know about conditions in Britain, but no one commented adversely on them.

Alba was dressed for travelling. She wanted me to compliment her on her outfit. Her boyfriend was due back from Eastern Europe soon, and she was full of it. I carried a bunch of roses. For the rest of my stay I would have to miss a meal a day – if you could call sawdusty scrambled eggs and near-black bread a meal. Still, there was any amount of fruit about the place: apples cost about two cents, and the hotel gave them away for nothing, and oranges too. We flew down to Camaguay on a Russian turboprop, taxying to the runway at near take-off speed. At the end of the runway the pilot made a turn to port so sharp that my roses, in their vase of water, went flying across the aisle. It is an interesting but useless fact that the

Poles in the Second World War used to handle aeroplanes in the same way. As a one-time flight mechanic I found myself shuddering for the undercarriage.

We were met in the protocol lounge by Manuel Correra, a party official. He had my vase refilled and ushered us into a car which would take us to a nearby hotel. I was going to have a meal! As I slavered over potatoes and beans and some kind of steak, Manuel filled in the missing details on my father's grave. For the first time I learned that he had not been buried in Santa Cruz del Sur, where he had been taken to hospital from the little port of El Guayabal, but in a place called Amancio, one hundred kilometres from Camaguay. We were to go there presently. In the meantime, Alba and Manuel wanted to know what I had been doing for the past few days, and their eyes showed their satisfaction on hearing my very positive mini-report on the working classes of Havana. After lunch we were on our way in a big, pre-war American Ford, sporting all the varieties of fairing and aerofoil flourishes of the period. These cars are as much a tourist attraction in Havana as are the gondolas in Venice. We tore through countryside given over to beef cattle and sugar cane. Every so often we would see a mechanical harvester, for the days of cutting cane by hand were over. To my delight we passed *caneros* on horseback, like figures straight from a Hollywood movie, straw hats pulled down over their eyes, lean, alert, on horses that looked surprisingly racy. In the villages through which we passed in clouds of dust, housing conditions looked grim as people sat outside rough shacks, watching us rocket by.

After an hour and a half we drew up in Amancio, named after an early socialist murdered by Batista forces in 1949. I was led into a building where a committee awaited. In general, I like committees. Some of my best friends belong to committees. I told this to the Amancio committee at the start of my speech of thanks and it went down quite well. It was chaired by a black lady. She poured orange juice for us at the outset. Then she handed out boiled sweets. The day before, I had also been offered boiled sweets by a civil servant back in Havana, and when I shook my head, I was urged to put it in my pocket for later. It reminded me of the Ministry of Agriculture back home: if a senior officer held a meeting with four or more present there was an entitlement to free tea and biscuits from the trolley. As a result, there was a minimum of four present at all meetings held, and the senior officer would urge us to take another biscuit, because they were free.

I told the committee that everything in Cuba had turned out beautifully, that the people and the officials had been truly helpful. The only thing missing, I said, was that the famous Teofilio Stevenson, the world's greatest boxer, was too busy working in the fields to meet the public. It was a good thing I knew my boxing, for a man on the committee engaged me in a knowledgeable discussion of the sport, into which I was happy to toss an opinion. It was a tribute to Alba that, knowing nothing about the game, she managed to translate and referee a good engagement between us.

Then the senior lady rose, with the others; I joined them, as, slowly, watched by silent, respectful townsfolk, we processed down the dirt street, to a building that had municipal written on every brick. The front door was open. A chair sat by a broad table. The leader beckoned me inside. I went in and sat on the chair; the others stood outside. I saw that a large register was open on the table. I put on my glasses and looked. There it was, in copperplate writing, in amongst the Spanish names, Mark McAughtry. My God, it was actually here that he had lain for thirty-two years, and not one of us to stand over his grave and mourn.

His name wasn't Mark, it was Marriott, a fine family name, popular in Carrickfergus in County Antrim, from where Mother's and Dad's families came originally, coaxed on to the mean streets of Belfast, when the city was doubling and redoubling in size, in the mid-nineteenth century. His shipmates had called him Mark, so that was the name on his seaman's discharge book. He had died at 10.30am on 6 October 1951. Doctor Oscar del Pino Diaz had been in attendance. Peritonitis poisoning.

Now I knew. He had died 2,500 miles from his family, making him the second of the family who had died far away from home, except that my brother, the other Marriott, wouldn't have his name in copperplate any-where. He was at the bottom of the North Atlantic, halfway between Canada and safety. There was a while when Mart's name appeared on the Roll of Honour of the War Dead in our church on Duncairn Gardens, but only for a few months: St Barnabas's Church was burned to ashes, and Mart's name with it, in the second air raid of 1941.

Alba beckoned me out, I joined the group and we went into the *cementario*. A discussion ensued as the committee tried to locate the grave. An old man was fetched: he remembered that foreigners were buried facing the east. In one such grave lay a Swedish seaman with a headstone; the other had to be my father's. There was only a crumbling wooden cross, no surround. The ground was black and hard and cracked. All over it lay the leaves of a giant casuarina tree. The committee turned away as I knelt beside the grave and closed my eyes. We Protestants don't go in for the repose of souls. I gave thanks to God for leading me here, to see my father's resting place at last. I scooped the hard earth away and bedded my cheap vase of roses.

I didn't cry at the grave. Anyway, he wasn't the crying sort. He was a dry-spoken little man who wouldn't talk if he had nothing to say. I was the only talking machine in the family. Yet he wrote the most beautiful love letters to Mother. I used to take them from behind the clock and read them. Each one began 'Darling Lizzie,' and ended with 'I am, your own, for ever, Marriott'. There followed lines and lines of kisses. After Mother died in 1946, home meant nothing to him any more. 'He was one of a breed that has almost died out,' his last captain had written to my sister. What the captain meant was that my father was one of the last to touch his cap to a ship's master. After Mart died, Dad's ship was due into Belfast after another nightmarish trip across the North Atlantic. On compassionate leave from the RAF, I was there when the *Dunaff Head* docked, and I was walking with him along the jetty when we passed Captain Finlay, the shore skipper of the fleet. Dad at once touched his cap and bade the captain good day. 'I was sorry to hear about your son,' the other said, and Dad actually shrugged and changed the subject. Clearly, he didn't want to load any of his troubles on to such an important man. That's what's called being the last of a breed.

I rose from my knees and the sun went in and the sky blackened. I said goodbye to the gentle and civilized people of Amancio. As we drove away the clouds turned purple and the rain battered down on the baked ground of my father's grave. I sat by myself in the back of the car and watched through the rear window until Amancio dissolved and finally disappeared, in the car's spindrift wake.

Back home it is 1986, and in the midst of the squalid murdering match which had been elevated by so many into a just war, I wrote a story that perfectly illustrated the true nature of the beast in Northern Ireland. It concerned Herbie, my friend from childhood. I met him one day on the Antrim Road with his wife, Martha, and I was delighted, as usual, to see them. I hugged him, shook his hand, kissed Martha, and was well into a volley of greetings, when Martha's signal stopped me dead. 'He can't hear you,' she said, 'he's profoundly deaf.'

It was then that I saw the expression on Herbie's face. There was no twinkle any more in his eye, and no smile lines on his face. His head was cocked expectantly, but his attitude was more one of puzzlement than the familiar mischievous, anticipatory grin that I remembered so well.

'He was beaten up, attacked,' Martha explained.

I listened in horror to the details as Martha told me what had happened. Herbie was a musician: in addition to the piano he could play the piano accordion, the clarinet and the guitar. This particular night he had been playing the electric organ in a working men's club in the centre of Belfast. He was walking home from the club in the early hours, when he came up to the junction of two roads marking the boundary between loyalist and republican areas. A dozen or so youths stood on each side goading each other; it was the classic overture to a clash. Made reckless by a drink or two, Herbie went over to one of the groups and suggested that they go across the road and shake hands with the lads of the other persuasion. It was close to insanity. Only an innocent like Herbie would have considered asking these fired-up bigots not just to be reasonable, but to be civilised. Martha would never know whether what happened next was carried out by loyalists or republicans, but the outcome would have been the same, whichever side he might have chosen. These were people who had sucked bigotry with their mothers' milk. He was over sixty years of age, but they set on him, using their clubbing fists and their feet. They kicked him unconscious, and even then they kicked him until he had stopped twitching and groaning. They wanted to kill him, and they would only have stopped when they were sure that he was dead. In the killing grounds of west and north Belfast the victim didn't have to hold an opposite political view to be assaulted. The one view most calculated to trigger an attack from either side was the liberal one: if you are not with them you are against them. The Good Samaritan Protestant boy who helped to clear the damage after a UDA bomb attack on the Falls Road was slaughtered for being there, as was the Catholic student

My father, Mark McAughtry, just up from the engine room on the SS *Dunaff Head*. His ship was torpedoed in 1941.

My brother Mart's ship, the *Kenbane Head*, sunk by enemy action in 1940

With Alba Holder, my guide in Cuba

My father's grave at Amancio, Cuba. 'A crumbling wooden cross, no surround. The ground black and hard and cracked. All over it lay the leaves of a giant casuarina tree.'

In 1981 with Lyrics Murphy who welcomed me to Ringsend to write my first story about Dublin. I lived for a year among these lovely dockside people.

At the RAF museum in St Athan, south Wales, in 1984, where I trained as a flight mechanic forty-four years earlier. The aircraft is an FW190, one of the enemy's most formidable fighters.

At the press
conference to
launch the Peace
Train Organisation
in 1986. Chris
Hudson is to my
left and Seamus
Lynch to my right.

On the roof of
Belfast City Hall in
1986 chatting to
Lord Mayor
Sammy Wilson.

The great Cyril Cusack concentrating on his lines
at the Bray Festival in 1987

The line-up for Barry McGuigan's first chat show in 1986.
From left to right: James Ellis, James Galway, the champ, and me.

In good company. From left to right: Conor Cruise O'Brien,
Gerry Fitt and Paddy Devlin in 1987.

At Ballnasloe Horse Fair for Moore Sinnerton's film company in 1988

A lovely moment with Paddy Devlin in the Kitchen Bar in 1993

Sharing the platform with Anne Tannahill of Blackstaff Press at the launch of my novel *Touch & Go* in 1993

Albert Reynolds in 1994 by the Shannon River. He was Taoiseach from 1992 to 1994 and helped broker the deal that led to the Good Friday Agreement.

In class company. I was awarded an Honorary Doctorate in 1998 at St Patrick's College, Maynooth. Dr Garrett Fitzgerald (front left) made the presentation.

who happened to be the handiest target leaving a south Belfast church on a Sunday. To stand aside from the murder was a capital offence in the minds of these republican and loyalist dupes.

Herbie owed what was left of his life to the fact that the attack took place within sight of the Mater Hospital in Belfast – an institution that had also suffered at the hands of bigots because of its Catholic ethos. Some passer-by alerted the Mater and for weeks the medical staff worked to help restore some semblance of life to their Protestant patient. He was discharged totally deaf, numbed and dulled mentally. When I last saw him it was in a nursing home. He remembered me. He even said my name. I don't know whether he understood me, but I told him then that I would always remember him for his lovely music, and for the good times we had together in years that we didn't know would be the most peaceful and innocent of the last century. It's true that, as someone has said, God gave us our memories so that we might have roses in December.

I was remembering the Herbie that I had known. He was so close to me that he had been the central character in the first story in the first collection that followed my first book. The story was called 'The Mutton Dummies' and has been included in an Oxford University Press school book called *Choices*. It tells of the time when Herbie invited me to his tenth birthday party, and of my great pleasure on receiving this invitation, for he and his four lovely sisters lived in a house that was three times the size of our little two-up, two-down.

My mother dressed me up as best she could, in a handed-down suit and a big brother's shirt with stitches at the neck to make it fit, and canvas shoes known as mutton dummies. They were torn and curled up at the toes;

Mother tried to compensate by applying whitening to the shoes and even to the outside and inside of the curled-up bit. I could live with the suit too big and the shirt too wide, but the mutton dummies bothered me: nobody else would have busted mutton dummies. Herbie's people were grand: their pictures appeared in the papers at posh balls and dinners; they wore evening dress. The boy guests would all have real suits and the girls would have lovely dresses. In this mood Mother kissed me, told me it would be all right, and I left.

I was no sooner out of the house than the rain came bucketing down, leaving the whitening behind on the ground in little swirls. I arrived outside Herbie's house but by this time I had lost my nerve and couldn't face the party, so I stood in a shop doorway from where I could watch the house and the party in full swing. Herbie and his sisters were sophisticated party-givers. They had the looks and the graces. Herbie himself was good-looking, with fair, wavy hair, a good physique and a bubbly personality. He had a bad stammer, but he laughed so much at his own efforts to talk that it was more a badge of distinction on him than a disability.

Once I saw Herbie come to the door and look up the deserted road: looking for me, I thought. As darkness fell it grew cold in the shop doorway. I saw young guests arrive, to be welcomed by Herbie or his mother.

As the party progressed I could hear the piano playing and singing and laughter: they were playing parlour games in the wide drawing room, and I could see their shadows on the blind. Trams ground past, the drivers, open to the elements, warmly wrapped up against the cold and rain. Finally, the door opened and the first of the guests left. The party was over. I ran down the street, taking a different route to avoid passing Herbie's door. By the time I reached home the stiffness was gone. I sat up to the fire, slipped off the saturated mutton dummies and warmed my toes. Mother was watching me closely. In reply to her question I told her that I had enjoyed the party very much. 'There's broth in the pot for tomorrow,' she said, still watching me. 'It'll warm you up. You look awful cold.'

'Broth? No thanks.' I laughed in disbelief. 'Broth? After buns and sandwiches and things at Herbie's party?'

Mother rose, kissed me goodnight, picked up her stone hot-water bottle from the hob and pulled herself up by the steep banister rail to bed.

In 1979, when the book that included the story was published, I was invited to Herbie's parents' house and they were all there, the son, the four girls, and the parents. We had a wonderful evening together, the first after many years of separation. We met up again occasionally, but when I met him with Martha that time on the Antrim Road in 1986, I hadn't seen him for a good six years.

In the late 1980s I introduced a little competition into my column in the *Irish Field*, Ireland's premier racing and eventing paper. For the three best racing stories I offered a free night's bed and breakfast at the Gresham hotel, transport to the Irish Derby, and free tickets into the reserved enclosure.

I awarded one of the prizes to a republican prisoner from west Belfast, who was serving time in Portlaoise prison. His father visited him once a month and in the course of the visit the prisoner would give his dad the names of three horses he fancied to win. His selections were good, because he had lots of time to work on them. His father missed one visit, though, which was a pity, because the three horses won. Later, the prisoner learned that the car carrying his father and brother-in-law to Portlaoise had been put out of action in a shunt with another car at Dundalk. The thing that had annoyed the prisoner, though, was that the other car was a police vehicle. I contacted his father, and he was delighted to take up the prize. However, he explained that he didn't drive and asked if it would be all right to include a son-in-law in the prize. I then wrote a short note to the driver: 'Come to the Gresham and ask for me'. We had a lovely time together, and when the Derby was run, the driver was the only one of us to back the winner.

A couple of weeks later I was at home upstairs, working alone, when the doorbell rang. Two men stood on the step. 'It's the police, Sam,' one said. 'Can we come in?'

I brought them in, sat them down, and started the coffee brewing, talking generalities until we were all sat comfortably. There was embarrassment in the opening remark.

'We're Special Branch, Sam, and we have a problem.'

'Oh, yes?'

'We've gone over this a dozen times and we can't work it out, you see.'

'How can I help?'

'Well, you see, it's like this. We were searching a house in west Belfast and we came across a letter behind the clock. It said, "When you come to the Gresham hotel, ask for me, Sam McAughtry." Now, we have studied this high up and low down and we give up. What's the crack, Sam?'

'Will you excuse me a minute?' I asked. They nodded. I went upstairs and came down with a photo. 'Is your man in that?' I asked. They picked him out right away.

'Where was that? Who are these other people standing beside him and you?'

I pointed. 'That's the manager of the Gresham, that's my friend, a Belfast man who won a prize in my racing competition, that's another winner, that's the father of a prisoner in Portlaoise who won the prize, too, that's his brother-in-law, who backed the winner, and that's me at the end, smiling.'

On the doorstep, one of them said to me, 'We never would have guessed that in a thousand years, Sam.'

'I was very nearly famous there,' I said.

'Well, put it this way – you were very nearly some-thing,' they said, walking out of my life, thank goodness.

Although my life has had more downs than ups, it has followed the sort of course that is well-nigh perfect for a writer. I had been near to death in childhood, had survived into harsh poverty, growing up in an even harsher loyalist political climate, with uncles and cousins who were nationalist. I had seen Lord Carson buried and heard the first divisive rantings of Ian Paisley. I had fought as a combatant in the Second World War, had been injured fighting a fire during Belfast's Easter Tuesday air raid in 1941, and was buried and dug out when the military hospital where I was recovering was bombed three weeks later.

The day after I kissed my mother on my arrival home from three years' overseas service, I was kissing her dead brow. I went to London and worked as a builder's labourer, living in dormitories with men on the run, and worked down deep sewerage trenches, making friends and swapping war yarns with German Luftwaffe prisoners. I worked on the Ford assembly line in Dagenham, where I was introduced to trade unionism, and then I came back home and got involved in the public service union movement, at a time when women had to leave the service on marriage, were paid at a rate lower than men, and were denied promotion to the senior ranks. I was involved in the struggles to right all these wrongs. Several years before the balloon went up in 1969 it was our own Catholic general secretary who vetoed an early attempt of mine to raise in the union journal the matter of discrimination against Catholics in reaching the top ranks of the civil service. Most Catholics were conservative at that time, believing that it was better to raise this subject quietly, discreetly, and without making big waves.

I also spent a lot of time socialising with journalists. I was a stringer for all the Belfast papers and a frequent contributor to the features pages. Unfortunately I didn't earn enough in this way to meet the then rigid National Union of Journalists (NUJ) membership terms. I was certainly better fitted for journalism than the civil service, and my NUJ card in later years brought a great calming of the spirit, but from the 1950s to the 1970s I spent many an evening satisfying my thirst with reporters, sinking pints poured, sometimes, by Gerry Adams, when he worked in the Duke of York bar, before he got involved with the people who blew bars up. In the early 1960s I joined the Northern Ireland Labour Party, and it was when the party lost every seat in Castlereagh Council in 1968 that I went out and ordered a glass of lager, and went on my final binge.

So the well from which I drew the stories which

launched me on *Sunday Miscellany* was a deep one indeed. The drinking yarns were so convincing that it caused real dismay when, particularly in Dublin, I was invited to have a drink and had to decline. But I was producing so many of these stories that, sometimes, people had to be reminded that they were only a pastime, that I could handle more serious material just as easily. In order to get the feel of republicanism I took to frequenting pubs in the heart of Provoland for part of my slant on the Troubles for the *Irish Times*. This wasn't a quarter as risky as a Catholic working from a loyalist pub, but it carried a bit of an old *frisson* just the same, especially drinking in the local republican club in north Belfast, being eyed up by tense-looking nineteen-year-olds.

In one of the many contradictions thrown up by the Troubles, there were two Protestant old-timers who refused to leave one bar just because the clientele had in 1969, almost overnight, become red-hot republican. Aggrieved Catholics who had been driven from areas where they were trying to integrate with Protestants had, in turn, driven the Protestant drinkers from the place, but this pair of pensioners had ignored all signals. They had their own seats and nobody in the bar argued about it. One of them, Alec, remembered me well from my growing-up years in what had once been a loyalist street only yards away, where walls that had once carried union jacks now carried the Republic's tricolour, and the rusty nails that had once anchored red, white and blue bunting (which I had often helped to string) now carried green, white and orange.

Alec was my conduit for local knowledge. Every once in a while the barman would call time on his bar bill and I would give Alec a hand to clear it, which gave me good standing behind the counter. In return, I was able quickly to become known and accepted by the company, although every now and again I would intercept a speculative glance from some of the younger drinkers with a look of active service about them.

Just outside the bar, on the far side of the road, there was an army lookout post surrounded by bullet-proof glass, around which were huge splash marks from paint-bomb attacks. Sometimes, tanked-up boozers leaving the bar would shake their fists at the camera on the pole and yell abuse at the hidden soldiers. One night, as I was leaving with Alec, to my astonishment he rushed out into the middle of the road, made faces at the camera, gave it the fingers, and told the watchers inside the post what to do with themselves.

'What the hell are you doing?' I asked him.

'What am I doing?' he said, spitting stout all over me. 'They were doing a search on the Hallidays Road, and they took a basket of loose potatoes off a neighbour woman of mine, spilled them on the ground and kicked them all over the place.' He shook his head. 'I didn't want to mention it in the pub, because I wouldn't give them fellas more to shout about, but that woman was near on to seventy, she has nothing to do with the whole carry-on, nothing at all.' He gave a final shake of his fist. 'I wore that uniform in the war,' he said, 'but I never thought I would see it used like that.'

I was reminded of an incident I had reported in the *Irish Times* in 1982. I had received a message from a community worker in the Short Strand, a republican area in east Belfast close to the UDA-controlled Newtownards Road, that an Ulster Defence Regiment (UDR) patrol, following a republican sniper attack from the area, had behaved in much the same way during a search of the Strand, roughing people up in the street, breaking up ceilings and searching for arms in working-class homes. This is army practice in any country in the world, in varying degrees, when soldiers are fired on and are being killed in a situation of civil unrest. Understandably, it is next to impossible to have this acknowledged by the civilians concerned. After the soldiers leave, all memory of the shooting that brought in the army in the first place is submerged; the damage to the area lingers in the memory and on the television screens.

In the Short Strand after the search, I met an old man in his late seventies who had been stopped by a UDR man. 'What's that you've got in the parcel?' he was asked. The pensioner explained that it was a piece of meat for his lunch. 'Oh,' said the soldier, 'well, let's see if it's meat or if it's bullets.' He then took the meat out of the wrapping, rolled it around in his grimy, cupped hands, and then handed it back. 'Seems all right,' he said.

This is what soldiers do: I had seen its effect many times in the post-war communist rising in Greece. And of course, there would have been nobody more delighted at the army reaction than the Short Strand IRA commander, who ordered the shooting in the first place, but I castigated the UDR section concerned in the paper, because it would have been wrong not to.

In the years to come, I was to be reminded of that condemnation by loyalists. It was seen as a betrayal of the UDR, whose men endured such suffering at the hands of hit-and-run Provos, but all that I could hope for was that the more thoughtful among the unionists would understand that the soldier who is allowed by his officer to humiliate the innocent becomes a recruiting officer for the enemy who is killing his comrades.

The British army could be just as brutal to Protestants when the situation called for it. For example, just before the different parties sat down in 1973 to discuss the formation of the devolved Sunningdale government, troops went on to the loyalist Shankill Road and laid about the locals, including allegedly breaking one woman's jaw with a rifle-butt. The army was attacked by Protestants, and soon the scene resembled a typical republican riot. When the Reverend Dr Ian Paisley arrived he was reported as saying that something very funny was going on, but later, when unionists sat down with nationalists at Sunningdale, as far as army support was concerned, their claim to the high ground was weakened. It might have been planned, or it might have been just a coincidence.

When the army appeared on the streets of Belfast in 1970 it was to protect Catholics from loyalist violence. At first the Catholics made tea for the soldiers, and there were even liaisons between soldiers and Catholic girls, but the very idea of good relations existing between British soldiers and Catholics represented anathema to the IRA, so they began to shoot soldiers, the squaddies went ape in Catholic districts and the IRA were ready to roll. This is a tactic from any terrorist handbook. Bring the troops in to relieve the civil power and moral balance goes straight into deficit. The biggest losers, of course, were the troops themselves. The time would come when the Provos would whitewash walls, the better to outline their soldier targets. As I escorted old Alec home to his tiny house I was thinking of all this, but what was the good of trying to explain it to somebody who had seen an old lady insulted, humiliated and frightened to death by someone whom she regarded as one of her own soldiers?

One evening in the bar I noticed a group of four men in their forties with their heads close together, in earnest discussion. They were talking in low voices. I thought to myself that it might, just might, have something to do with the IRA. At the time I was trying to chair a theological debate going on between two brothers, fuzzy on pints, on the subject of whether or not there was a God: 'Who do you think made the stars, eh? Tell me that, for fuck sake?'

I went to the bar, standing as close to the four men as I could, and looked into the mirror, whistling soundlessly, with my good ear cocked towards the conversation.

'I'm not gonna do it,' one was saying.

'You're gonna have to do it.'

'I'm not gonna do it, and the more people that do the same, the better.'

(This guy wants to leave the IRA, I thought. He's showing a hell of a lot of courage.)

'You have no say in the matter. It's been decided at top level and that's that.'

'Is it? Well, we'll see about that.'

(Nerves like steel.)

Then I heard the clincher. 'No matter what you say, St Joseph's is finished as a church. We'll all have to go into St Patrick's parish.'

They were actually talking about the closure of a church in Dockland.

I wanted to introduce the atmosphere of the pub to my readers. As I carried the drinks to the table I decided to lead with the church closure story after all. It wasn't a race between that and 'Who do you think made the stars, for fuck sake?'

*

Maeve Binchy once told me that the most significant contribution I had brought to the *Irish Times* was the fact that I had never tried to be a Dubliner, but that I was always the visitor, outside, looking in. It is true that no matter how much I love Dublin, I have never thought of settling there. I once rented a house off the Malahide Road for over a year and every few weeks a nice man would call at my door on behalf of the local church. He would chatter away about church matters – sodalities and the like – never knowing that I belonged to the faith which, as Cardinal MacCrory once famously announced, was not a part of the church in Ireland, and was not even a part of the church of Jesus Christ. I would give the man money, if it was needed, and shake his hand, and agree that it was one kind of an evening or another. The children in the avenue learned my name and the little girls, playing outside on a summer evening, would knock on my door and shout through the letter box, 'Sam! Your taxi is here. Sam!' But I never did what my mother used to call 'neighbouring'. Even at home in Comber, where I have lived for thirty years, although lots of people know me, I don't know the names of many of my neighbours, and the only group with which I socialise is the Republic of Ireland Aircrew Association. So maybe the habit of watching and recording from a distance is in my nature.

Francis Stuart said more or less the same thing as Maeve Binchy the first time I met him, only he said it in a defensive way, at the launch of his book *Faillandia*, in Dublin, in1985. This was eleven years before a blazing row developed over a proposal before Aosdana, the elite affiliation of artists created by the Irish Arts Council in 1983 under the chairmanship of Anthony Cronin, when he was arts adviser to the then Taoiseach, Charles Haughey.

The proposal was that Stuart be elevated to the rank of Saoi within Aosdana.

The main objector was Maire Mhac an tSaoi, the wife of Conor Cruise O'Brien, based on the fact that Stuart had gone to Germany in the war and had broadcast material which had the approval of the Nazi regime. By the time I met Stuart he would have been eighty-three years of age, but his faculties were still sharp. The speeches were over when I arrived at the book launch, but he came to the edge of the crowd and shook my hand.

'You know,' he said, when the greetings were made and I had wished him well with the book, 'you are an outsider too. You are here in Dublin for new experiences, just as I was when I went to Germany. Any writer worth his salt must leave and search for experiences that differ from those of his own country.'

I had then only a superficial understanding of Stuart's background. I replied by laughing and saying that the Germans certainly offered new experiences to me without the asking, by trying to shoot me down thirty-seven times in the air and blow me up twice on the ground during my RAF career. He laughed. 'I know,' he said. 'I know what you mean.' He, too, had had a chancy time, at the war's end, when the Allies were looking into the nature of his relationship with the Nazi authorities.

Stuart had fought in the Irish Civil War, had been captured in an ambush and imprisoned. He had married the daughter of Maud Gonne, had had a play staged at the Abbey Theatre, and another taken off after public protests. He looked the part: tall, handsome, in the Elizabethan way. He imagined that his self-expulsion, as he called it, was meant to remove him from the stultifying effects of bourgeois morality, but his claim to have been in Germany just to be different is undermined by certain anti-Semitic letters that he wrote to the papers. He had to take a good deal of flak, but at least, in the last weeks of his life, Dublin's literati honoured him, even though he was too far gone in senility to appreciate the gesture. Meanwhile, whatever about Stuart's links with the Nazis, nobody anywhere in the Republic seemed concerned by the fact that, walking the streets of the city, were wartime IRA men who had been happy to run to the Nazi ambassador to Ireland and report the damage done to Belfast, where a thousand Irish were killed in two air raids in 1941. Dublin is a very interesting city for the man on the touchline.

In a book by Professor Brian Walker, *Dancing to History's Tune*, the author points to a good many examples of the misuse of history, and, since Ireland and history go together like Siamese twins, the following quote from the book might be appropriate. It is a lift from a work by A.T.Q. Stewart, the distinguished northern historian, and it goes, 'To the Irish all history is applied history, and the past is a convenient quarry which provides ammunition to use against enemies in the present.' Various experts confirm, writes Walker, that the actual study of history, North and South, falls below the average of countries in Western Europe. And Professor Joe Lee, of Cork, pointed out at a Merriman Summer School in 1993 that less than a quarter of students in the Republic took history, a smaller proportion than the norm elsewhere.

In my own experience, a typical example of the everyday Irish way with history was provided in 1983, when a press photographer, a man who seemed pragmatic in every other regard, told me that when his son brought home a new pair of trainers, he ordered the boy to return them to the shop at once, because they had been made in

Hong Kong and had tiny union jacks on the heels. 'We've had enough of the Brits in the last eight hundred years,' he said.

The history need not be ancient. When the Troubles were young, many unionists boasted about their wartime service with the British, in order to prove their loyalty. Chief among these was the late, egregious Johnny McQuaid, MP, a loud Shankill Road unionist, who once boasted to the House of Commons, which, at that time, included many decorated British MPs, that he had parachuted into the jungle with the famous Chindit forces in the Far East. Behind him, in the Labour benches, Gerry Fitt, now Lord Fitt, called out, 'He must have landed on his head.' Gerry himself had sailed on merchantmen on the highly perilous Murmansk convoys, and said nothing about it.

Paul Tansey was features editor at the *Irish Times* and Olivia O'Leary was a political correspondent on the paper when I worked with them in D'Olier Street. They fell in love and were married, and about a year later I happened to broadcast a little piece about the role of the father of the bride, here summarised:

It is my daughter's wedding day. When her mother and two sisters have left for the church Marion and I are alone, in the suddenly quiet house: what do I say to her?

I have no trouble at all in addressing audiences of hundreds, or talking to radio or television audiences of tens of thousands, yet I don't know what to say to my first daughter on the happiest day of her life. She looks lovely. 'You look lovely,' I say. She smiles nervously, plucking at some part of her bridal gown. If I had only thought to write something down beforehand, I could say it now, but all that I said next was, 'You're getting a lovely day for it.'

The car arrived outside, and I still hadn't told her that I loved her. 'I love you and I am happy for you,' I said. She smiled a dutiful smile and I realised that women talked about loving people all the time. The word that was causing my voice to shake and my face to turn red was everyday talk to her. The door was knocked and we left. I wanted to kiss her on the cheek in the car, but it would likely spoil some of her make-up, or something.

The wedding speech by the father of the bride? Money for jam: 'Other fathers say that the parents of the groom have gained a daughter, but in our house I say that we have lost a daughter and gained a bathroom.'

After the honeymoon the happy couple arrive at our house. When she comes in I rise and offer her the chair that has been mine and holy ground for all the years that she was growing up here. Her mother and I rush to make tea for them and for the rest of her life she will enter this room as a distinguished visitor, dearly loved.

A few days after the broadcast I received a note from Olivia which read, 'One day Paul and I will see our child leave us to marry. Thank you so much for your lovely memory.'

Every now and again, when I've read a letter, instead of dropping it into the wastepaper basket, I put it into an old cardboard box in my workroom. All my nicest memories rest there and Olivia's sweet sentiment is in good company. I have a little decorated note from Maeve Binchy in this box, sent to me from hospital, where she was in pain after an operation on her back. She wrote that an RTÉ story of mine had made her laugh for a while, as she pictured the tale. The story was about the time my brother Tommy, aged thirteen, mitched from school for six solid weeks, during which time he and his chum Happy Matchett were cleaning up at a card school while I, aged ten, on Tommy's instructions, was telling the headmaster that my brother was gravely ill. What eased Maeve's pain was the picture that I had painted of thirteen-year-old Tommy offering loans at interest to the men he had skinned at the cards.

It was around 1987 that BBC Radio Ulster introduced *Talkback*, an hour of political debate. In the beginning this programme, devised by Martin Dillon, an original thinker, was extremely worthwhile, primarily because it gave our local politicians as much airtime as they needed to make their points. In presenters Barry Cowan and David Dunseath and with Dillon at the helm, the show attracted a huge audience, by the North's standards. I was one of the founder-contributors: my six- or seven-minute spot was on Wednesday mornings, and I was followed by Eamonn McCann, one of the hardest-working journalists in Ireland. McCann had been an early supporter of Sinn Féin, but his left-wing politics were of an older and more global pedigree, and gradually he has eased away from a purely Irish republican stance to the kind of selfless, dedicated international socialism that has long had my admiration, even though my support runs mostly to buying their news sheets.

I enjoyed the first couple of years on the programme, largely because Martin Dillon gave me leeway every so often to introduce listeners to the theatre of the absurd, which, in my view, is an integral part of the backcloth to the green–orange clash. The fun pieces went clean over the heads of the more humourless partisan listeners. One of them rang in to say that McAughtry sounded like 'a tuppenny book with the back ripped off'. I wondered if the anonymous caller was influenced by the poet Craig Raine, who wrote that seeing Belfast from the air was like seeing a transistor radio with the back ripped off. I wasn't displeased.

The most biased comments came in from listeners who refused to identify themselves, other than by forename. The practice of letter-writers hiding behind pen-names is endemic in Northern Ireland, and the papers do little to stem it. There are rare areas of debate where a pen-name would be essential, but the North's morning and evening papers have for many decades gone along with the practice when, as the *Irish Times* and the English broadsheets have shown, an editorial ban on pen-names, except in special cases, results in a much more thoughtful and interesting standard of correspondence. With the *Irish Times* the first page that many readers turn to is the letters and editorial page but with the *Belfast Telegraph* and the other northern dailies the readers surely must turn to this page last. So I wrote a piece for *Talkback* dealing with this phenomenon, considering its origins, and inviting debate on the proposition that this preponderance of pen-names was a sign of a politically sick society. It came as no surprise when the talk was pulled, I assume, on the grounds that the programme relied on bigots such as 'Sean from Poleglass' and 'Tommy from Ballysillan' to stoke up the heat. So I resigned from *Talkback*, after three years. I had never considered the possibility that I would feel like the one outside, looking in, even in my own homeland, but that's the only way to describe my reaction at that time. Years later, I felt that I wasn't alone when I heard Gerry Anderson, who hosted the programme immediately preceding *Talkback*, say, 'Cheerio, folks, it's time to listen to the Crazies.'

I was well used to the sound of sniper fire long before the Troubles broke out in 1969. I had been through a curfew situation in 1935, when Belfast republicans reacted to the triumphalism of unionists as they celebrated the Silver Jubilee of King George V. There had been rioting and violence throughout 1934, with loyalists attacking Catholic homes in the York Street area, and things came to a head on the evening of the Twelfth of July 1935, when republicans clashed with an Orange procession returning from the Field at Belmont. A trivial enough incident developed into a full-scale shooting match on York Street. To my mother's alarm I was there, at the edge of things, eyes wide and mouth open. The army backed up the police in the north Belfast area and I saw the Whippet cars opening fire in warning bursts with machine-guns, and felt nothing but fierce excitement as my mate Herbie and I, both twelve-year-olds, peered around shop doorways, learning within minutes to tell the crack of the sniper's rifle from the revolver's bark.

My fifteen-year-old brother Tommy was out playing football after the 9pm curfew and was led home by a beetle-browed, loud-voiced RUC man. Boys of the same age were helping the republicans, the angry policeman told Mother, so he'd landed Tommy home in order to prove that he had given the correct address. I was listening at the kitchen door, and I heard my mother plead with the peeler not to summons Tommy. 'He's a very good boy, Sir. My boys are all in the Church Lads' Brigade, and Tommy is a corporal, so he is, Sir. Don't be lifting him, Sir.'

I remember feeling a rising resentment at Mother's surrender of her dignity. The feeling was to become familiar in the years ahead, and was to lead me into trouble whenever I imagined I saw rank being used to humiliate.

The 1935 violence lasted for some weeks, resulting in a dozen deaths of Protestants and Catholics: two thousand Catholics were driven from their homes. Herbie and I were thrilled by the nearness of the action. It was all around us. Once, our family was sitting in the house when the sound of a revolver made us jump. It was coming from the entry at the back of the house. Before Mother could stop me I rushed through the scullery to the yard and peeped out of the yard door. Our house was near the top of the street. The revolver's bang echoed against the narrow walls of the entry, and I saw a man kneeling at the opening. He was looking left, towards the Catholic New Lodge district. After firing another shot he glanced over his shoulder and I had only time to note the wicked grin on his face before Mother grabbed me, pulled me back into the yard and gave me a slap across the face, but to this day I can still see the grin, and the man's broad backside.

Herbie and I were bouncing a ball against a wall in Lepper Street the next day, when suddenly the spouting on the wall in front of us broke into tiny fragments and the sound of a rifle followed in a split second. We darted off in different directions. Next day in school we held our mates spellbound as we described the near-miss. I told them how Herbie's stammer had disappeared like magic, as we swore in a blind bloody panic. But it was thrilling, too.

Fifty years later, in 1985, not far from Lepper Street, I found myself in a doorway once again, as bullets flew. An RUC Land Rover was the target. This time the weapon was a republican machine pistol, and the bullets were hitting the pavement and the road. I was reminded that bullets send up sparks when they strike stone or metal. There wasn't much of a thrill about it then, but I wasn't frightened either. If you're in a shop doorway you're all right, provided you don't stick your head out. A poor woman in Hillman Street did that, in 1921, and she got one right through the head.

Like half the population of Belfast I've seen umpteen bombs go off, but from a hell of a safe distance. When I was in the clinic in 1971 we patients used to stand at the window of the ward after hearing a city centre explosion; we would study the plume of black smoke and pinpoint the location.

'It looks like about North Street,' said a binge drinker, once.

'Could be the Red Hand Bar,' opined a man who used to be chief steward on a cruise liner.

'Or, alternatively,' I said, 'it could be the White Cross, next door to the Red Hand.'

'I hope it's not the Red Hand,' said a man who had us all puzzled, because he used to go on the tear for just one month every year, then he went off it again. 'I certainly hope it's not the Red Hand, because they've got priceless old variety bills there from the Alhambra Theatre that was.'

'Well,' said the chief steward, 'I hope, for one, that it is the Red Hand, because one of the bills there is mine. I owe them fifty quid.'

My usual day working for the *Irish Times* in the north Belfast office between 1981 and 1987 was pretty undramatic. It was not in the least like those of the hard news reporters. Amongst *Irish Times* northern editors Henry Kelly was one of the most articulate of these, both in print and on television, and Conor O'Clery was the most cerebral. Both had left the Belfast post when I joined the paper, Kelly for full-time radio and television work, and O'Clery was on his way to international recognition as a respected commentator in Russia, China and the United States.

Before I went to work in Dublin Henry Kelly and I joined in a broadcast one Twelfth Day from RTÉ's studio in Belfast and it was a delight to work with him. It was such a pleasure, as we sat watching the Orange procession, to be able to move into surreal mode and have it bounced back to me like a brand-new shuttlecock. Henry, as is well known, was always fond of a bet on the horses, and once, in bookie Sean Graham's box at Cheltenham, watching me signal my bets to Brian Graham from the veranda, Kelly was curious as to the strength of my betting. He was dying to know if two fingers meant two hundred pounds and Brian refused to tell him, citing bookie–punter confidentiality. I backed three consecutive winners that day; in fact, my stake was twenty pounds on each. I won about three hundred quid, while Henry frowned and wondered for a while whether it was three thousand, and if he was in the company of a heavy hitter in his own league.

For a few years my name was on the list of guests invited to lunch or dine with the secretaries of state at Stormont or Hillsborough Castle. The times when local colour and good gen regarding our Balkan-style thinking were wanted from journalists were the most interesting. Once, when I was seated beside Secretary of State Tom King at Hillsborough, one of the security correspondents was airing his knowledge of paramilitary goings-on, dropping big names all over the soup and fish, even down to their love lives, their sexual preferences and the vengeance of cuckolded killers. For Tom King it was all very complicated. He was a nice chap, not at all devious, and when, well into the main course, we were treated to a colourful tale of homosexual carry-ons featuring two Provos, King turned to me and muttered, 'It's all so arcane.'

'You don't want to bother about the half of this,' I whispered back, 'these guys love to shoot the shit.'

'Mmm ... yes,' said the Secretary of State, but he looked as if he would much rather have been Minister of Agriculture instead. Of the few British ministers that I met I think

I liked Tom King best. He was an uncomplicated man, one of the few who, when his stint in Northern Ireland was over, didn't go around acting as if he'd been the last man out of Saigon. Close to him I would place Richard Needham, one of the best ministers of state, who had a genuine love for Ireland, and who did more than any other politician to create the new and elegant Belfast of today, built on the rubble left by the Provos.

My family weren't all that happy about my working in and around the New Lodge area, but for most of the time I was easy enough in my mind about working in a place where the most disadvantaged on either side of the peace line were so full of hatred. There was a great reassurance in my having been brought up in these streets. I walked as if I owned them, but a cousin of mine, on the Catholic side of the family, was walking up the Cliftonville Road early one morning in 1985 when a car came to a halt beside him and a man with a gun in his hand pushed the door open.

This cousin was a bright guy, just short of his fifties. He'd been a fair amateur boxer and a good soccer player, and he'd kept himself reasonably fit, but even so he was lucky that the gunman fumbled the opening of the door. Instead of turning and running Sammy hurled himself at the car, pulled open the door, jerking the gunman forward, then he let him have a fourpenny one on the whiskers, before running off as hard as he could, across and down the road to safety.

I told myself that it just went to show that nearly everybody in working-class Belfast was marked in some way by the Troubles, but a particular burden was carried by families whose members crossed the mixed-marriage line. For all that I knew the gunman in that car might well have belonged to a family from nearby Tiger's Bay that I would once have known and respected. Further to complicate the Rubik's cube, another man whose relationship to my family was more distant became a dead Provo folk hero, big time, big mate of Gerry Adams, killed by the army in 1973.

When I first came to Dublin I was surprised at the unreserved approach of some of the writing fraternity. A much-loved writer stopped at my table in Bewley's café on Westmoreland Street, chatted for a bit, then suddenly said, musingly, 'I'm a better writer than you are, but you're a better wit.'

I told him that he was pushing an open door.

Another writer was one of the tiny group that I called the Saloon Bar Brigadiers – comfy down in Dublin shouting 'Charge!' to the IRA from a range of one hundred miles. A well-known Dublin biographer, poet and playwright seemed not to think of himself as such, but as a hard man. He boxed amateur, and was just about the only educated gentleman boxer I've ever met who liked it to be widely known that he could use himself. At least it's a change from the usual one of the pugilist wanting to write poetry, but it clearly turns this guy on.

On another occasion when I was having a coffee in Bewley's, a slightly built man dropped a little note on my table as he passed on his way out. He had gone by the time

I had read the note, which said, simply, 'Welcome to Dublin, Sam. It's nice to have you here.' It was signed Michael Hartnett. Michael died in 2001. He was a lovely poet with an awesome gift for translation from the Irish, and, with equal ease, from Hungarian to the Irish. He had the genuine humility that goes with the gift of writing elegant poetry. The last time I saw him was at a mass book-signing for charity in Ballsbridge, approaching the millennium. He was tired and very ill, but all that he wanted to talk about was what I'd been doing since we'd last met.

Douglas Gageby thought of his next big idea as we were lunching in the Royal Hibernian hotel with a retired major general from the Irish army who had served with Douglas during the Second World War, or what they call the Emergency in the Republic. The general and I had lots in common: he had done time in the Signals during his service, and I had recently broadcast a story about the days when Morse code was in use in communications between air and ground.

This story is a true account of how I took a crash course in Morse code after arriving in London in January 1942, for the first stage in flying training. It was then I learned to my horror that we would be required to take dot–dash messages, and that failures were out of the race for good. Other than the sequence for SOS, I knew none of it at all, but suddenly I remembered having somewhere seen a book, *Teach Yourself the Morse Code*, and I ran to the nearest bookshop, in Swiss Cottage, and bought a copy. I had twenty-four hours to learn it. Its method was to substitute words and phrases to imitate the Morse sound for each letter in the alphabet: for example, the letter Y, sounding like dah-dit-dah-dah, was represented by the phrase 'You Can Do Yours'; for Q, dah-dah-dit-dah, 'God Save The Queen', and so on.

A sergeant wireless operator announced that he would start at four words a minute, and then the buzzer began to spit out the symbols. To my great surprise I found that I could transcribe them perfectly. The buzzer was talking to me. 'God Save the Queen', it was saying, 'You Can Do Yours' and 'X Marks the Spot'. I handed in my message sheet with a broad smile. Three candidates were failed and dropped out.

'Now,' said the officer in charge, 'we'll try six words a minute.' Away went the buzzer, and it didn't bother me one bit. 'Chase Me Charlie', it said, and I wrote C on the page; 'Freddie's Freezing', it went on, and I chortled as I added the letter F. About six more hopefuls bit the dust. For the ones that were left the officer said he would try eight words a minute. Try away there, I said to myself, it's all one to me. All through my life I had grown used to being good at useless things, like holding my breath for well over a minute, and playing the bagpipes. This was yet another exotic talent to add to the list. I only just managed to get a decent score at eight words a minute, and the officer beckoned me to a corner of the room. 'You are just what we're looking for,' he said. 'You're a dab hand at the Morse.'

'But I'm trying for navigator,' I said.

'I know,' replied the officer, 'and you're going to go forward as a navigator, plus wireless operator, plus gunner as well. We would like you to blow ships up, in daylight, in aeroplanes with two-man crews. We need you badly. Are you pleased?'

'Why do you need me badly?' I asked suspiciously. Nobody had ever needed me badly before. He just smiled enigmatically. I learned later that the enemy were shooting anti-shipping aeroplanes down like bloody flies.

While the three of us were swapping service yarns, Douglas suddenly said to me: 'Why don't you do articles on the three arms of the services here?' And so I found myself watching army recruits square-bashing in Phoenix Park, and I went on a patrol with operational soldiers at Dundalk, whose quarters, like those of the British army in the North, were dog-rough. I formed a theory then that hard lying, as soldiers call it, could be one of the reasons behind rough handling of civilians by soldiers in all countries where they operate in war conditions. Live rough, eat rough, act rough.

Major incidents just before I arrived at Dundalk were the murders of thirteen RUC personnel by the IRA, nine of them mortar-bombed in their barracks in Newry, and four killed by a landmine. In the Republic, a Garda sergeant was murdered in Tallinstown while pursuing armed robbers. I went out with a patrol led by a sergeant from Belfast's Andersonstown. Visible on the other side of the border was a British army lookout post at Forkhill, County Armagh. I hated it as much as the republican residents in the North, but not for their reasons: for the thousandth time, I felt anger at the sheer stupidity and incompetence on the unionist side that had led to this potent symbol, and its huge propaganda significance for the Provos.

The visit to the Irish Air Corps at Baldonnell was an altogether more pleasant experience, because here, for all the progress that had been made technologically since I had left the RAF Reserves, I still spoke the language and understood the culture.

I was taken on my first helicopter ride in an Alouette over Brittas Bay, round by Blessington lakes, across the Coronation Plantation to the Sally Gap in Wicklow, to Lough Tay and back to base. The pilot was Captain Andy McIntyre from Donegal, specially chosen, I suspected, to make me feel at home with the tongue. The Air Corps had saved over three hundred lives since 1964, I learned, but our second passenger, a photographer from the *Irish Times*, worried about his life rather a lot, especially on hearing my request to the pilot just before take-off. 'Let's fly very low and very fast,' I'd said, and Andy did, to marvellous effect for me, but it ended when I received a mighty dig from the photographer, and a reminder that he wasn't into this kind of carry-on at all.

I finished the day with dinner in the officers' mess, with Colonel Pat Cranfield (now a retired brigadier) at the head of the table. It was a splendid evening. I was presented with the Irish Air Corps tie, which I wore subsequently at a function attended by the Reverend Dr Ian Paisley and lots of his friends.

I had deliberately left the navy visit to the last. When I walked up the gangway of the patrol ship *Eithne*, I was indulging in a boyhood fantasy. I had haunted the Belfast waterfront as a boy, hoping for a dockside jump on a short-handed tramp steamer, and it never happened. I had been on board dozens of ships anchored in Belfast in my teens, and I had sailed as a passenger on troopships across the Atlantic and back, including the *Queen Elizabeth*, but now I was going to have the run of a ship, from bridge to mess to engine room. *Eithne* was new in every detail, she smelt of fresh paint.

On the bridge I watched the captain, Jack Jordan, con the ship quietly and with no fuss until we reached the open sea. We stopped a trawler, but it proved a nil report: no arms meant for the Provos, no illegal haul of fish, no swarthy illegal immigrants. Down in the wardroom it was cosy. We drank gallons of coffee; I met Paul Keaney from Carnlough on the Antrim coast, and the other officers sat respectfully listening to us discuss the agony of our homeland. I turned in at two in the morning to my roomy cabin and fell asleep pretending that I was master of a cargo ship homeward bound for Belfast from Montreal, just passing Belle Isle.

We tied up at Dun Laoghaire harbour at noon; I said goodbye to the officers and felt rotten having to refuse the traditional whiskey on berthing. I was met by Captain Declan Carberry, the army public relations man. As we walked along the jetty, an Alouette clattered overhead. At the moment of finishing my defence forces survey all three arms were with me. That was nice.

It was around this time that Tony Breen died (this was not his real name). He was a highly intelligent drop-out, in his early fifties, from County Tyrone. I had come to know him through the witty postcards he sent to me. Tony lived in scruffy lodgings on the north side of Dublin. I used to call and take him out for a meal occasionally, but one afternoon when my knock went unanswered a neighbour told me that the landlord had increased the rent, Tony couldn't afford it, his belongings were dumped in the street, and Tony had thrown himself into the Liffey and drowned. I stood in the street and cried. That's another side of life not particularly confined to Dublin.

In the late 1980s Dominic Behan invited me to take part in a television show on RTÉ. It promised to be fun. The format called for a celebrity to entertain guests of his or her choice. Previously, the honour had gone to Paisley, who had brought with him his family plus Sammy Wilson, an over-the-top Paisleyite. Most of the population of the Republic had watched, hypnotised, as though they were seeing caricatures of the whole Protestant people of the North, but this was something else. I was delighted to have been invited; the other guests were to be Spike Milligan and Larry Adler, the writer and harmonica-playing genius.

I had never met either guest; naturally, I was dying to appear with all three men. More than anything, though, I wanted to meet Spike Milligan. I was a big admirer. At that time my headquarters in Dublin was the Gresham hotel, so, on the big day, when I learned that he was booked into the same hotel I couldn't wait to ring him up. I was about to behave like a raving fan. That well-loved voice was saying hello.

'Hello,' I said, 'I just thought I'd ring you up.'

'That's what you've done, all right,' came the answer.

'My name is Sam McAughtry.'

'Is it?'

'Erm ... I'm one of Dom Behan's friends. I'm on the show this evening.'

'Yes, and ...?'

This guy was a wall of silence. By now I was in splindereens.

'I wondered ...' (What the hell was I wondering?) 'I was wondering if we might share a car to the TV centre.' I was looking at myself in the wall mirror. I was pale and sweating. I had a rictus instead of a smile.

'Look,' said Milligan wearily, 'I know I'm in Ireland, but surely to Christ the cars here are big enough to hold more than one passenger.'

I hung up without replying. Now I resented him. Up Milligan's chuff. I had read that he suffered from migraine, but I wouldn't have treated a fan like that if I'd been in the last stages of the clap.

Later, downstairs by the desk, Milligan was dressed in one of his show costumes: red, with a little-boy jacket and a big, floppy bow. All across the lobby people were craning their necks. Catherine on the desk introduced us: I stayed two yards back from him and nodded, distantly. He waited in silence for the courtesy car to arrive, while I chatted cheerily to the porters and the concierge. When we got into the car I sat in front and he climbed into the back. On the way the female driver kept up a cheerful flow of conversation, sometimes pointing out sights: not a word from Spike. 'That's a new nursing home,' the girl said.

'A short course in there would do your man in the back seat no harm,' I said, not bothering to keep my voice down.

Then I immediately felt sorry. I turned and began to praise Dominic Behan and told Milligan what an honour it was to appear with him on the show. When we arrived we were both relaxed. He even told me that I had 'a good aura'.

Once on stage he was wonderful. So was Larry Adler. It was almost uncanny to hear Adler's recollections of Hollywood in the 20s and early 30s; of his friendships with Chaplin, Buster Keaton, Lillian Gish, Clara Bow, Jean Harlow, Laurel and Hardy, and many more of the stars who had enthralled me as I sat as a kid in the York Street fleapit. Some years after his appearance on RTÉ, I was to interview Adler for the BBC in his flat in London. After about an hour of his wonderful conversation he rose and apologised for bringing matters to an end. 'I have a date to play a lovely lady at tennis,' he explained. He was almost ninety at the time.

In March 1984 Rinty Monaghan, the popular north Belfast boxer, died. He had held the world flyweight title at a time when, unlike today, the world champion was the world's best. He was certainly a one-off. I was beside him at a Belfast Celtic versus Cliftonville football match in the 1950s. It was winter and there was a fair depth of frozen snow underfoot. A fat, red-faced RUC sergeant patrolling the ground appeared in front of us, beside the touchline, and suddenly a hefty slab of snow and iron-hard ice sailed over the fence and nearly carried his head off. At my feet, the champion of the world was down and out of sight, winking at me and laughing like a drain. The crowd closed tighter and the sergeant had to give up the search. Another typical Rinty jape had been pulled.

He died aged sixty-four. I went to his funeral mass in St Patrick's Chapel on Donegall Street. The place was packed with Catholics, Protestants, Jews and also-rans. Towards the end of the service the priest said something that I couldn't hear, and the man beside me reached out and took my hand. I thought he was a fan, so I said: 'How are you doing? Isn't it desperate about poor Rinty?'

The man was looking dumbstruck. A lady on the other side of me pulled her hand back after trying to offer it to me. I had started to talk to her too about Rinty, until someone behind me told me that I was just supposed to say: 'Peace be upon you,' or something like that. Behind me a group of Catholics from North Queen Street were laughing their heads off. I could swear I heard Rinty's laugh as well.

In December 1984 I travelled over to Yorkshire to report on the nine-month-old miners' strike. Arthur Scargill, the fire-eating President of the National Union of Mineworkers (NUM), had taken over from wise old Joe Gormley. Scargill announced right away that the days of pandering to the management were over. This personal grudge against Gormley seemed to colour many of

Scargill's actions from the start. Another feature of his strategy was to talk as though he represented 'his class' in Britain, and not just the miners.

In the days before the strike was called in March, the Tories were openly baiting Labour MPs at Westminster, reminding them that the power stations had a year's supply of coal, and if this wasn't enough to withstand a long strike, arrangements had been made to import coal from Europe and the USA. Scargill seemed unable to recognise the trap that had been set for him, and, without a balloted mandate from his members, he went ahead and called the strike. His spiky attitude had previously lost him friends in the trade union movement, but once hostilities were opened the unions got down to the long haul of helping the miners and their families, against a government which had started by denying social security payments to the families of strikers.

A majority of Nottinghamshire miners refused to go on strike, adding considerably to the hardship of the strikers, although strictly speaking they were not blacklegging, since they had not been asked to take part in a ballot.

The television appearances of Scargill versus the pro-government spokesman soon indicated that the latter's claims regarding the number of mines affected by the closures policy were greatly understated. Arthur Scargill said time and again that the Thatcher plan was to destroy the industry, a forecast that proved to be well founded. Unfortunately, his leadership on the ground was immoderate, which, in turn, allowed the government, in a move that smacked of fascism, to bring police forces from the far end of the country to drive through Margaret Thatcher's policy of humiliating all the unions, through the NUM, and breaking their power for good.

Such tactics drew support from other countries to the British miners.

Scargill was slow to condemn wildcat behaviour by some of his flying pickets, resulting, in one case, in the death of an innocent motorist whose car was struck by a breeze-block dropped over the parapet of a bridge by a young striker. Scargill's own general secretary was openly at odds with him over the matter of culpability in this incident.

Thanks to Bill Blow, a Yorkshire-based journalistic colleague, I was able to move in with a mining family in the pit village of Wombwell, near Barnsley. The old terrace house faced Darfield colliery over sour, starved ground. I was staying with Marcia Marshall and her husband, Spud, one of the striking miners. For the whole of my stay there the police were referred to as pigs and bastards by the miners and their families. In the Wombwell area the police were from Norfolk. At dawn, the morning after my arrival, I joined a crowd gathering to protest at the arrival of scab workers in an escorted bus. Upon hearing my accent among the crowd a police inspector called me out and demanded to see my identification. I showed him my NUJ press card. He glanced at it and then asked me where I'd come from. I told him Belfast, then I asked him where he came from, remarking that it certainly wasn't Yorkshire. As an answer, he turned me around, put his knee in my back and gave me a mighty shove back into the crowd, to loud jeers and catcalls from the audience.

The withdrawal of benefits from the miners' families gave rise to the worst hardship I'd seen since the aftermath of the air raids on Belfast in 1941. Although relief was coming in from many parts of Europe, as well as Ireland, communal meals prepared in the various miners' halls contained largely basic ingredients. Some idea of the effect of the strike on money values in the community was brought home to me when, on the third day of my stay with the Marshalls, a daughter arrived and I was regretfully asked to move. Spud rang around the pubs to book a room for me; he listened for a bit, then he lowered the phone and shook his head. 'I'm sorry,' he said, 'but it'll cost you ten pounds a night B&B. I can't get it any cheaper.'

In the pub where I was staying a reporter from the Tory-supporting *Sun* newspaper approached me. He was tracking Scargill and was trying to get a lead on whether the strike leader was pocketing money sent for relief purposes. The local word was that I was on the inside track with the Scargills. A fruitful lead and there would be a bob or two in it for me. The reporter was clearly disappointed when I told him that Ann Scargill's wage for working in a Co-op shop was supporting the family. I also passed on to the tabloid the information from the front line that a miner's wife had been strip-searched and thrown into the cells for approaching her husband on the picket line. The journalist wasn't the least bit interested. He wanted to know from me if I had any information regarding a house that Scargill's soon-to-be-married daughter was to occupy.

Scargill was suspicious of the press, but through Marcia Marshall I was introduced to Ann Scargill, and through her I had Arthur's ear. I put it to him one evening that I couldn't understand why he kept saying that he was fighting for his class. 'That is the job of the politician,' I said, 'your job is to fight for your members.' He didn't reply, he just gave me a look that said there was no point in trying to explain it.

I went back to Wombwell a year later, to see how the

families were faring over Christmas 1985, in the after-math of defeat. Thatcher was in the USA boasting about how she had licked the unions; the Nottinghamshire strike-breaking miners were in the dole queue as well, for their loyalty, the industry was facing wipe-out, and Arthur Scargill was making fiery speeches to a tiny union membership. An old miner in Wombwell gave me my closing line. 'Defeated peoples pay reparations to the victors,' he said, 'and for atonement we are giving Thatcher our Christmas.'

In 1989 I scripted and presented a television programme produced by Roger Green called *St Patrick's and the Tiger*. It was set in the loyalist Tiger's Bay area and the republican New Lodge Road, in north Belfast, both areas coming together at Duncairn Gardens. The purpose was to show Protestants the plight of Catholics living in over-crowded conditions, in an area where housing lists were very long, jobs were hard to get, and the priest and curates of St Patrick's Chapel on Donegall Street spent their time counselling, and helping the women of the parish to get through their day. I asked Gerry Fitt, James Galway, Frank Carson and Brian Moore to come on board and all four adjusted their diaries to help.

I asked a wise friend who lived in the area to do some research for me on the nationalist side a week before filming. I needed background on St Patrick's Chapel, on the location of recreational centres and on the names of local figures who would need to know that I would be walking the streets there, and who could talk to me on local issues. After an hour on the task my friend phoned me in some embarrassment to say that he couldn't go on with it. 'Sorry, I can't take it,' he said. 'Certain sections here are not happy about your part in this. I don't want to get mixed up in politics.'

On hanging up the phone I dropped everything, drove over to the New Lodge, parked the car on North Queen Street and began to quarter the district. I knew in my heart that the people in my old neighourhood wouldn't object to me.

In the old days, although the neighbours in our street were mostly Protestant, we had given our business to Catholic shop owners, and even the local moneylender had been a Catholic lady of impeccable discretion. I went first of all to the place which, for generations, had been the meeting place of the workless – the betting shop. There would be the odd young Provo there, maybe even the odd older one, but if I was going to be challenged it would as likely be here as anywhere else. It was the first day of the Cheltenham Festival, the place was pleasantly full, the teens and twenties were there in numbers. I went up to the counter, struck a bet, went back and sat on top of a meter-box to watch the race. I hoped to be loudly recognised and it didn't take long. A man of about twenty-five spoke to me: 'Aren't you something on TV? Tiger's Bay?'

'In a manner of speaking,' I said, as breezily as I could, 'you could say that I invented Tiger's Bay. It was only three or four streets when I wrote about it, and now it seems to have spread along dozens of streets and roads.'

He had the set look that showed he didn't much fancy the topic, but we were interrupted by a man in his forties.

'What do you fancy here, Sam?'

Gratefully, I dropped into racing talk.

'What has you over here?' he asked, after a bit.

'I'm making a film here next week,' I said, noting the interest being shown by those nearby. 'It'll be about St Patrick's parish.'

I watched the race with the rest, crunched up my docket and high-kicked it, then I went out into the autonomous republic of New Lodge and began to talk to people on the streets about the film I was going to make. I visited the church, the boxing club, the leisure centre and the primary school, where the headmaster told me that the children knew all about me from a school history book, and that the one thing they knew about me best of all was that I hated school. I stood at street corners and spoke to young lads and I bought sweets in wee shops and told the owners about my film, and finally I spoke to one of the priests of St Patrick's. He was most helpful, but one comment he made was indicative of the Church's attitude to the left-inclined Workers' Party. He readily gave me details of Sinn Féiners who might be worth notifying of my intentions, but when I mentioned the Workers' Party he said, 'Yes, there's a nest of them on the New Lodge Road.'

Three hours after arriving, tired and ready for the road, I reached my car on North Queen Street. As I put my key in the door a young fellow who had been leaning against a wall came over to me. 'Are you the man who's making the TV thing round here?'

He was about nineteen. Just the dangerous age. I was ready for objections and I was ready to tell him that Cardinal Daly had approved the notion of the film when he said in true Belfast style, 'D'ye see the pub round that corner and down that street?' I nodded. 'Well, the man that owns that pub says for you to call in when you come here and he'll give you your lunch.'

The year 1989 saw the unveiling of Barry McGuigan, the 1985–86 World Boxing Association's featherweight champion, as a chat-show host. Barry was nervous about this, his first television exposure, and I agreed to open the show as first guest, to be followed by James Ellis, the popular actor, and James Galway as the star guest. Jimmy Ellis is a friend for whom I have written a number of radio dramas and it was hoped that he and I would settle Barry's nerves and help him do a good job.

By this time I had appeared on many television shows, without being troubled by nerves, but this record had a near squeak on *The Barry McGuigan Show*. I took my seat before his entrance, he was announced, and appeared to resounding applause, gave the boxer's salute, took his seat, read the introduction from the prompt and turned to me after announcing my name. As God is my judge, I have never in my life seen such naked terror in any man's eyes since the war. This is a guy who feared nothing and nobody in the ring, but the signals that were jumping from his eyes that evening nearly did for me. I had to take a deep breath, then I found myself saying, 'There you are, now, you've been on air for a full minute and you haven't made a single fluff.'

He laughed, the audience laughed and I was telling myself thank God for that. He went on to complete his first chat show and when it was over I felt like towelling him down, he was so whacked. In a subsequent programme he said to George Best, 'You know, George, you're my greatest fan.'

It can happen to the bishop. The only reason I mention it is because Barry was such a complete warrior in the ring, such a devastating puncher, that I expected him to dominate the studio in the same way. As this is written he has found his true metier, giving commentaries at boxing matches on Sky television, where he has a vocabulary and an assurance unmatched by any of his contemporaries. In addition, by his efforts in the field of fighters' welfare, Barry McGuigan is on the sort of high ground last occupied seventy years earlier by world heavyweight champion Gene Tunney, the most intelligent boxer ever to hold a world title.

I was to meet James Galway a number of times when I was presenting television and radio programmes. He is immensely popular at the National Concert Hall in Dublin. Always, of course, in the Republic, there is the northern Protestant factor. They know our honest, decent side, and they love to see it. Galway has on stage a calm, natural, friendly aura that the southerners see as a welcome antidote to the noisy haranguing so often associated with unionists. When the President of Ireland is in the audience, and Galway opens the show with the 'Soldiers' Song', the applause that follows owes as much to the player and the significance of the occasion as it does to the presence of the head of state.

In 1989 I went to the Greek island of Corfu for a holiday. It was a lovely holiday. I went for a cruise around the Dodecanese islands; we went ashore at one or two of them, but we didn't get off at Samos. I didn't mind. I knew a number of Greeks on Samos, but I stayed on the boat, and here's the reason why.

Four years earlier, in 1985, the media were marking the fortieth anniversary of the ending of the Second World War. Since I was the only journalist around D'Olier Street who had served in the war, I was sent to do my own kind of memoir. Later, the journey formed the basis of a book, but for the anniversary I set out to return to some of the places where I'd been stationed. I went to St Athan, in south Wales, where I'd trained as a flight rigger, then on to Cranfield in Bedfordshire, to a pilots' training school where I'd worked as one of the ground staff. When the aircraft were in the air we mechanics had nothing to do, so I wandered one day into the classroom where the cadets learned navigation, compasses, magnetism and other flying skills. After a couple of such visits the education officer gave me a test and suggested that I could handle a navigator's course. I applied, was accepted and, thanks to the *Irish Times*, here I was again in the places where I'd served as a nineteen-year-old. Really, though, I only wanted to visit two overseas places for the series: the first was Mount Hope in Ontario, where I graduated as a flier, and the other was the Dodecanese island of Samos. The budget didn't run to Canada but I visited Mount Hope later.

The airport on Samos is five miles from the town of the same name. My taxi drove up the main street of Pythagorou, where Pythagoras was born, then we climbed a steep right-hand turn, and there it was in front of us, a deep blue bay, a high hill dense with vegetation to the left, a jetty, and a pretty village at right angles. There was a beautiful peace over everything; this was Samos. I had last seen it through the grey, black and orange of anti-aircraft fire from harbour and ship defences, and the white trails of our sixty-pound rockets converging on a German minelayer.

'I've been here before,' I said to the driver. 'I helped blow up a ship at the jetty in 1944.'

The driver's eyes widened. 'They still talk about it here,' he said.

Some of the rockets had missed and had hit the waterfront. Each was equivalent to a naval six-inch shell, but Guiyot Marc, the British vice-consul, told me that I needn't worry. 'You will be a celebrity,' she said. Then she advised me to go and visit Manolis Panayaris, who lived on top of the hill. 'He knows all about the bombing,' she said.

Manolis, at that time seventy-five, was a great character, with lively eyes, and a powerful fondness for the Greek wine retsina. When the interpreter told him who I was he embraced me, and nearly knocked me drunk with the fumes. He lived with his daughter in a house with a beautiful garden and a magnificent view of the village below.

'I was the one who saw the ship coming up the creek,' he said. 'I radioed the British with the news. We invited you to bomb the ship, so don't worry.'

Manolis had no idea how speedily the RAF reacted to such sightings. From receipt of the message to take-off was only a few minutes. The flight to Samos took just under an hour. As the strike force breasted the hill, Manolis had just arrived at a taverna beside the harbour to tell all who would listen that, in an hour or so, they would see some fun. He was blown into the arms of the doctor's wife, or at least that's the way he told it, and the doctor's wife was more upset by that than by the bombing. The villagers were sorry to note that the ship appeared to have withstood the attack as a company of German troops marched on board to be posted to another island. But just about when we were touching down on our desert airfield near Gambut, on the Libyan coast, a smouldering rocket detonated the ship's cargo of mines. Many Germans were killed, but the only Greek casualty was a baker's boy of thirteen, who was delivering bread in response to a summons from on board.

I left Samos after VIP treatment on the island. Our shipping strike was only one of many such operations. None of our aircraft was lost. I had only wanted to go back there because I remembered the peaceful picture of the island from the air. For an instant, over Samos, before the attack, I had forgotten war and danger and destruction, and I had seen beauty and serenity. Then we had done our job, finished off an enemy ship and killed plenty of Nazis. But we hadn't been sent to kill the baker's boy.

I was invited to come back for a longer stay, but I didn't take up the invitation.

I eventually revisited Mount Hope in 1997, when I was invited to address the Canadian Association for Irish Studies at the University of Toronto at Mississauga, Ontario. To tell the truth, the opportunity to see the place where I had graduated as an RAF flier was half the reason why I had accepted the invitation.

Jim Russell, a post-war immigrant from Belfast who had prospered in Canada, took me to Mount Hope airfield, which was by then a wholly freight concern. When the people at reception learned of my background they welcomed me most warmly. Fifty-five years had passed since I had studied there, an early school leaver among college boys and graduates. There had been a number of failures among our number on the navigation course, and I remember on graduation day feeling absolutely euphoric, not just that I was going to fly, but that it was proof that I wasn't a blockhead. The schooling that I'd had in Belfast was meant to turn out unskilled workers who could count and write and know enough to carry out orders but not enough to question them. History has not adequately highlighted this positive element of a war that caused so much grief and destruction. An enormous change was wrought in the men and women with similar beginnings to my own who served in the armed forces. They learned to extend their vocabularies, to stretch their minds, and to match their wits with those alongside them who'd had better starts in life.

James Callaghan, who held the three great offices of state in Labour governments, and achieved the highest office of all, prime minister, served in the war as a seaman in the Royal Navy. On discharge, he became interested in trade unionism as a civil servant with the Inland Revenue, and through the union movement he came into Labour politics. All across these islands men and women with only elementary education returned from service to enrich society to a degree that would have been undreamt of six years earlier. This was first evident when the ex-service veterans threw out the Conservatives in 1945 and elected a government in Britain that would give all of the people in the UK an equal chance in health, education and jobs. The old, lackadaisical civil service in Northern Ireland, with its Orange links, Freemasonry, its Plymouth Brethren, the marriage bar, and its unequal pay and promotion structure, didn't know what hit it when a new breed with the task of administering the new benefits took their places. At Mount Hope they asked me what I was thinking when I stood quietly in the place where I used to read my books, cramming meteorology, trigonometry, logarithms and astro-navigation. It would have taken too long to explain to them that it wasn't the flying, but the great feeling I'd had when I'd passed the exams. For the college boys the passing was forgotten almost as soon as the lists went up, so I'd kept the feeling to myself.

'I knew a girl here called Gladys,' I told them, for the

record. 'She wanted me to fail my navigator's exams, stay here and marry her. I had a basic trade as flight mechanic, so I would have been kept on in Canada as part of the ground staff for the rest of the war. The price was too high, but it was the lucky man who got her.'

When Douglas Gageby retired and Conor Brady took over as editor of the *Irish Times* in 1987, I knew that my time on the paper was going to be short. Conor O'Clery had gone to the Russian bureau to file his brilliant reports on the dissolution of the Soviet system, Olivia O'Leary had gone to television, Paul Tansey was off to the *Sunday Tribune* and Bruce Williamson had retired. Brady didn't have Gageby's profound interest in the North and nobody was thinking up novel slants for me to explore. The fun had gone out of it. The news from the North would not be lightened up any more, but I left the paper on excellent terms. I had loved every single moment of my time there, and it was an honour to have served with such talented journalists. I left with only one regret: that, like so many before me, I had been unable to present a picture of my Protestant neighbours and friends in a way that would do them full credit. They had paid a heavy price for their political representatives' smug assumption that the Tories would balk any attempt to bring them to account for their handling of nationalist complaints. The unionists' 'powerful friends' in government had melted into the shadows. After Edward Heath prorogued Stormont in 1972 the unionists' truest Westminster friend, Enoch Powell, set them on a blind-alley course of total integration with

Britain. He didn't understand the British psyche: namely, that pleading to be British invites comparison with the Maltese or the Gibraltarians, or even the West Indians, who, under British colonial rule, went to the barbers to have their hair straightened.

At the heart of the Protestants' problem is nationality and culture, and culture can be a powerful public relations weapon. I cannot understand why the bulk of Protestant people whose breed have been here on this island for hundreds of years refuse to acknowledge their Irishness. They are not settlers. It would not only make for more ease of mind, but where the two Catholic parties are concerned, it would also be shrewd politics. Meeting Catholics equally on cultural ground would work wonders in community relations. This would not involve loss of face, nor would it signal a desire for a united Ireland. Just because Sinn Féin make so much noise about Irish culture is no reason to believe that all who claim to be Irish are nationalists. Over the last thirty years I have met hundreds of Protestants who share my convictions, including Chris McGimpsey, the unionist politician.

The culture is ours as well as the IRA's. Instead of rising like trout and claiming a Scots language which is treated with derision by most Protestants, we should be criticising Sinn Féin for debasing our common culture by using it for dubious political ends, and reproving those in whose care the welfare of the Irish language rests for lacking the guts to protest. To all outside the island we are Irish. It isn't a bad tag to have. To be Irish is to be interesting. To claim Scotland as the mother country is to make listeners' eyes glaze.

In the Opsahl Report *A Citizens' Enquiry*, published in 1993, my view was recorded as follows:

As a Protestant who has never had a problem in embracing my Irishness, I have been aware for many years that this single gesture brings with it more warmth and goodwill from Catholics than any other Protestant response within the context of our divisions. Given this, Catholics are prepared to accept that, my Irishness notwithstanding, I prefer to live under the United Kingdom system of government.

I should add to that the fact that there are a million Irish in Britain happy to follow the same cultural path. Neither Sinn Féin nor the SDLP like to face this apposite reminder.

Among other things, the Opsahl Report includes the following from my submission:

> It is sad to claim Britishness as one's culture. There is no such thing as British culture: the people in Britain are either English, Welsh or Scottish. It is equally sad to claim that one is an Ulsterman or woman, yet not Irish, since Ulster is a province of Ireland ... everyone but themselves see Protestants as Irish. They go into any serious negotiations a goal down because of this ... It would be a tremendous political gain for them [Protestants] to encourage the spread of Irish culture within their own community. At one stroke it would earn them a new respect from constitutional nationalists, making for a more tolerant climate (overall) and it would remove from Sinn Féin one of its most potent weapons, viz., the inference that unionists are settlers, mongrels, outsiders, aliens, Brits.

It was against this background that I met with the Protestant people who had been my neighbours and who had grown up with me in the Duncairn/New Lodge area of north Belfast. I had no more direct contact with their children than I had with the republicans of the same age on the other side of Duncairn Gardens, but when I was there in the late 1980s I found that many of those Protestant boys had served their time in gaol and had forsworn violence.

All through the Troubles the Tiger's Bay area was used by loyalist paramilitaries from other parts of Belfast as a starting point and a safe haven for raids across the line. The actual numbers of Protestants living there were few, and they included a great many older folk. When asked by me to justify the attacks on innocent Catholics, the loyalist paramilitaries referred firstly to the consistently heavy electoral support for Sinn Féin, even in the wake of the most murderous activities of the IRA, and secondly to the IRA's boast that it could protect Catholics. The loyalists' mission was to show that they couldn't. As for the residents, as I sat in the homes of the old folk and saw pictures of Paisley on their walls, knowing their poverty, I wanted them only to understand that I was as resolved to stay under a Westminster government as they were, but to them, some of my broadcast views had come across as green in colour. Sixty years of listening to political abso-lutes had obliterated all memory of Labour's concern for a century past on behalf of the disadvantaged on both sides. But it's hard to describe the sadness I felt when I read in the papers the familiar surnames of loyalists arrested for drive-past shootings or worse. I had known their parents and grandparents; good and decent people.

As far as the men of violence were concerned, as everybody knows, the contrast between both sides couldn't have been more extreme. Compared to the linear structure of the Provos the loyalists were like the warlords of Afghanistan – one boss to every square mile, just about.

Reactive politics can never truly form a noble cause. Their intelligence was leaky and safe houses were few and far between. The scorn among the Protestant middle classes both for Orangeism and for loyalist paramilitarism, and the absence of middle-class input was evident in the poor public relations performances of both. In the first Assembly election, the two Ulster Volunteer Force (UVF) representatives scraped home and the UDA failed to get a single candidate into Stormont, which is possibly why its political front collapsed in 2001, causing localised civil wars and sectarian attacks to erupt in loyalist areas.

M y next venture was into radio and television presenting. I enjoyed the latter because I wrote the scripts,
but interviewing guests on a radio show can be done by
practically anybody who has a decent vocabulary and
who bothers to research the subject, so long as the
interviewer doesn't try to upstage or lead the guest. On
British national television the use of comedians and other
celebrities to front chat shows, while it provides comedy,
has taken a good deal away from the original intention of
the chat show, which was to offer viewers an insight into
the lives of interesting people. Originally, I wanted a live
show with prominent guests and questions from the
listeners. My background covered such varied territory
that I could have handled politics, social issues, trade
union matters, literature and most other topics of the day,
but the programme manager saw me as someone

corralling in their hotel rooms celebrities who were over in Belfast for major concerts. In this way I often spoke to folk singers and recording artists about whose work I knew next to nothing, nor did I wish to learn, but the challenge for me was to nudge the subjects away from the press handouts and get them to talk about their concerns outside music: their early years, the kind of society in which they grew up, how they viewed Ireland, and their second loves in the arts. Singers painted in their spare time, actresses wrote screenplays, orchestra conductors went to jazz sessions, ballet dancers loved to jive, and they all had different preferences in literature. These were the really interesting aspects.

I remember one occasion when the lovely Kate O'Mara was in Belfast playing in *Antony and Cleopatra* at the Grand Opera House. She had promised my producer a morning interview, but when we reached the Europa hotel she refused to see us, because she had slept badly the previous night, wasn't in a talking mood and, anyway, she felt that she looked a sight. After a good deal of pleading she agreed to let me talk to her, having learned of my age and the discretion that it promised, but she wouldn't hear tell of the younger sound engineer or the producer being present. After more negotiations Miss O'Mara said that she would retire to the bedroom to let the engineer set up the recorder; he would then leave it running, I would enter, and she would see how it went after that.

She came out of the bedroom at my invitation and she did look tired, but otherwise gorgeous; I knew better than to mention either aspect, though. 'I know exactly how you feel,' I told her, when she was seated. 'I have been plagued with insomnia since I was a child.' Which was true. I told her about the long nights in my youth in the forces, when all around me others were sleeping like babies while I lay staring at the ceiling of a hut or the interior of a tent. I told her how, for most of my life since, I have to rise out of bed and tiptoe downstairs in case I wake my wife, and how I sit reading with my eyes burning until two and three in the morning, when sheer exhaustion would give me perhaps three more hours.

We sat and talked about ways to overcome the condition and she laughed when I told her that my favourite method is to pretend that I am in a submarine in wild Atlantic weather. Conditions are so bad that the captain decides to take the submarine down until it reaches a depth where all is calm and still. Then I lie in my bunk, happy that we are safe and sound, feeling sorry for the mariners up above who can't go deep for sleep; I close my eyes and keep my fingers crossed that I won't be awakened by a depth charge. She burst out laughing and we were off and running.

I got a lovely interview from Kate that morning, she even talked about a lost love, and I left her smiling and hoping that our relaxed interview would help her to snatch another couple of hours before lunch.

When I did a show with Robert Robinson, the urbane host of many radio and television shows, I had the opposite experience. He had left university with a reputation as a promising writer, but settled for the material rewards of television. When I mentioned quite objectively that the press were raising this issue upon the publication of a recent novel by him, Robinson became defensive, and I had to work hard to get a good half-hour out of the interview. I wasn't all that happy about it, since, some months earlier, I had done him a big favour, setting up a radio programme in Belfast for his radio series, which involved assembling a very entertaining team of guests. By contrast, one of the loudest and seemingly most garish performers on the box, Jimmy Saville, proved to be a most understanding and helpful interviewee. But the highest point of this period in my life was when I interviewed Sir Ludovic Kennedy, and he remembered my first book.

I remember one occasion when I had wound up a radio programme recorded in the Group Theatre in Belfast and the producer left without telling either the research lady or myself the name of the next guest. All that we had was his address. Two hours later we turned up at his house to interview him, went inside, and after the recording gear was set up I said to him: 'Now, just to see how it comes across to the listeners, would you announce your name and tell them what you do.'

'I'm so-and-so and I'm a farmer,' he said into the mike.

I shook my head. 'I didn't come here because you're a farmer,' I said. 'As a matter of fact I'm not struck on farmers, so just please tell the listeners why I have travelled eighty miles to interview you.'

'I'm so-and-so and Sam has travelled eighty miles to interview me because although I'm a farmer and he's not struck on farmers, he's struck on me because I collect old auction posters and various historic items that reflect the history of this place, and Sam has also forgotten my name and why he's here, hasn't he?'

Another odd start to an interview came once when a famous West Indian cricket knight came to Comber in County Down with his celebrity countrymen. I asked him for a few words at the Comber cricket pavilion and he lit on me like a ton of bricks. 'Can't you see I'm just off the bus? I haven't even had a drink yet.'

He was furious. I was annoyed. I shrugged and walked

away. 'Doesn't matter,' I said, 'forget it.'

He ran after me, keeping up his protests. 'You're right,' I said, 'I'm on your side. Can I go now?' He caught me at the door, pulled me to one side, and gave me a cracking interview. Young broadcasters note: only try this when you can afford to do without the money. If you're skint it won't work.

Through my early work in the Labour and trade union movements, my writings, and my work on television and radio, I used to tell myself that I was helping in some small way to bring common sense to bear on our troubles instead of emotion. Nevertheless, when I met community workers who were toiling virtually without recognition in republican and loyalist areas, trying to bring comfort to victims and their relatives, and to the families of prisoners, I was aware that, by comparison, writing and talking and making films were easy ways to make a contribution. When I had finished whatever I was doing I went back to my leafy avenue, parked the car in my quiet drive, and went into a house that didn't need its windows boarding up or its letter box sealed against petrol bombs. So when I was asked to chair the Peace Train Organisation (PTO) in 1989, I jumped at the challenge. It would be something to look back on with more satisfaction than was afforded by an Atlantic of ink or a mile of film footage. This would put my head above the parapet. Sinn Féin and the DUP would dislike it, each for their own reasons, but good could come of helping to end the bombing of the Belfast–Dublin rail line, and it would give me an opportunity to do something for the line over which I had made so many lovely, anticipatory journeys.

A group of politicians had met in Dublin to discuss ways of combating the IRA attacks on this vital link between Ireland's two capital cities. The bombings and warnings had been taking place for several years but had become serious in 1988 when the service had been disrupted on 172 occasions, and had already caused one fatality and several injuries. The meeting accepted a suggestion from the then Dublin TD Proinsias de Rossa that a special train, to be known as the 'peace train', should run from Belfast to Dublin and back, bearing representatives of as many sectors of Irish society, North and South, as it would take to drive home the message that the bombing had to stop. It was hoped that many prominent figures in Ireland would be included in the demonstration.

Paddy Devlin had proposed to the meeting in Dublin that I should be asked to chair the organisation on the grounds that I was not a politician, my Labour axe was too weak to be ground, and that I was an experienced media man. I knew nothing about all this, but when Paddy landed at my door with the details I was happy to accept: indeed, I was eager to start. Nothing could have suited me better. I was possibly one of the best-known travellers on the route, as a trade unionist I was concerned for the jobs of the rail workers, and finally, I had been messed about more than most by the stoppages and the illogicality of the tactic, plus the frequent delays to my journeys on the line had led me to worry some faint hearts in the *Irish Times* when I labelled the IRA in my column as the 'Brains Trust'.

The founders had asked Chris Hudson to chair the

Dublin committee of the PTO. Chris was an official of the Dublin-based Communication Workers' Union; he and I had never met, but when we did it looked like perfect casting. Chris came from the same sort of jumbled-up background as myself: he had tried being a postman, a boxer and an actor before reaching senior rank in the union movement. He had converted to the Protestant Unitarian faith, while loving his granny, who drew an old IRA pension. Chris was a fine speaker, with a sense of humour liable to break through at the most unexpected times. He also had what was vital for the success of the new project – a following in Dublin and a grip on networking that would guarantee a packed train from there, never mind what we could do in the North.

The Belfast committee was made up of so many clued-up members that it was a privilege to be counted as one of them. They included seasoned civil rights campaigners like Paddy Joe McClean, councillors, Ulster Unionists, members of the SDLP, Alliance and Democratic Left, Quakers, and Westminster figures like Lord Fitt and Harry Barnes, the Labour MP who stayed true to the PTO's principles even beyond the life of the organisation. The expertise at the first committee meeting was so advanced that only the one session was needed before we were ready to meet the press.

On the day, looking over the seated rows of journalists, I was conscious of the trust given to me by the committee in allowing me to handle the press conference in my own way. I had certain ideas as to how to approach it, while remembering that the press corps would, if I let them, pull me on to the favourite ground of the terrorists – name-calling – to see what would happen. I had witnessed it a hundred times on the television.

Modern media practice calls for the political reporter to throw a curve at the subject, no matter how far on the side of democracy and decency the latter might be. If the result is a gaffe by the interviewee then the reporter is a goal up and to hell with the consequences. Politicians accept it, but with no constituency to curb me, I didn't fancy it a yard. I began by announcing the time and place of departure of the peace train, then I gave our reasons for the protest against the attacks on the inter-city line, deliberately using one of the IRA's favourite terms; they liked to talk about their Protestant fellow-Irish, so I said that their actions were preventing me from meeting my Dublin fellow-Irish. I made a point of saying that I was addressing the IRA directly, and not its front men in Sinn Féin. I asked the organisation to reply directly. It had consistently claimed to be an army, subject to military organisation and discipline, so I was going to treat the IRA as such. I asked for a military reason for the bombing of the line, since it only tied down a handful of soldiers; and I asked for an economic reason for the tactic, since goods normally carried by rail would reach their destinations by road, and the end result would not have the consequences for the economy to compare with the shops and business premises burnt and bombed by the IRA. Finally, I asked for a political reason for cutting off the primary route between Belfast and Dublin, since the stated aim of the organisation was to unite the country, not split it in two. Here I described the Dublin grannies I'd met so many times coming to Belfast to buy presents for their grand-children, and the thousands from the North who travelled to the South, many for the first time in years.

Chris Hudson spoke next, expressing similar sentiments from the southern point of view. His trade union credentials were evident as he charged the IRA with directing its campaign against the working class. Our two voices, pure Belfast and Dublin, were new at this level of politics and peace, and Chris, an original thinker and fine speaker, complemented my contribution perfectly, as he reminded the IRA that Dublin had as much say in the matter of their bombing campaign as Belfast. He also mentioned, with a smile, the religious and political blend in his family. Listening to him, I was delighted. I glanced over at Paddy Devlin, Chris and Michael McGimpsey, Seamus Lynch and the other seasoned politicians along-side me, and I could see that they, too, were well pleased with how things were going. The all-Ireland image being projected provided a unique and telling way of announcing the launch of the PTO.

When the time came for questions my little private theory was put to the test. I was ready and willing and one of the Sky reporters obliged: 'Why do you pay the IRA the compliment of recognising them as an army when they killed a child in Germany only recently?' Indeed, and that was true. Automatic fire directed at an RAF man had killed a baby in the back seat of his car. The deed was so vile that it was very difficult to dodge, as the Sky man well knew, but to condemn it would only move me on to ground that was familiar to the IRA. The wartime bombing of Dresden would be down for the old whataboutery debate: it was territory that gave the terrorists any amount of cover.

I simply stared at the reporter for a moment and then said: 'We are here today to talk about the bombing of the Belfast–Dublin line, and why I am being prevented from meeting my Dublin fellow-Irish.' That was it. The rest of the press conference went well and we got worldwide coverage. It was bad news for the Sinn Féin propaganda machine. Their response was hesitant and in purely public relations terms it was one of the worst performances of their war. They offered the mixture as before – what about the closing of the border roads, the prevention of good nationalists from visiting their families' graves? There was no military justification offered, just, 'What about the army searches in nationalist areas?' The nationalist *Irish News* was supportive, using in its editorial a quote from my speech: 'Even using the IRA's convoluted thinking,' I had said, 'no sense can be made of the bombing of the line.'

In the days leading up to the first journey of the peace train I happened to meet up with a prominent peace worker who had been active for years ahead of me. In the course of a discussion with a third party present I said that when the work of the peace train was over, I intended to move out of the spotlight. 'I have no wish to become a permanent feature on the peace landscape,' I said.

I was astonished at his reaction. He was furious, clearly taking my remark to be a criticism aimed at full-time peace workers. 'There are a good many people who would feel hurt at that attitude,' he said.

In the years to come I was to learn that words had to be chosen carefully within the broad northern peace movement. Some who had been a long time on the scene seemed curiously thin-skinned. In fact, there was more going on in their minds than peaceful thoughts. The peace train was getting a huge amount of media attention, and to a few it might have seemed like a stunt. I appreciated that, and hoped that the political clout of our committee would ease doubts of that sort. Meanwhile, I was to be kept nearly as busy in the times ahead in sorting out differences between peace workers as I was in keeping the organisation well oiled between runs.

When the day of the first appearance of the peace train came I was almost dumbfounded at the response. At my right hand was the awesomely efficient Seamus Lynch, who, knowing my bad memory for faces, whispered into my ear the names and status of the many prominent people who had turned up to travel to Dublin. We had bishops, ministers and clergy of all denominations, except perhaps the Free Presbyterians – Dr Paisley hadn't been in touch with us. There were politicians, but no Sinn Féin or DUP. Sporting figures were there, actors and artists, poets, prose writers, composers and playwrights. I referred to the support of these artists later that day in my speech replying to the Lord Mayor of Dublin's welcome in Connolly Station. Unlike the men and women who fought in the Republic's War of Independence, I said, the Provos had no poets – or none worth the mention – in their ranks, or among their supporters.

During the journey to Dublin I walked the length of the train along with Paddy Devlin and Chris and Michael McGimpsey, the brothers who had obtained a ruling through the Irish Supreme Court that Articles 2 and 3 of the Constitution of Ireland amounted to a territorial claim on the North. Eileen Bell of the Alliance Party was also with us; she had a long record of working for peace and I was hoping that I might have her help on the administrative side of the organisation between peace train journeys. We shook hands with travellers all the way along the carriages and I marvelled at the number and variety of people from right across the religious and social spectrum who had come to support our demonstration. Certainly there was a gala air on board, but the passengers weren't there just to see the lines cleared: the desire and commitment to a fair and just settlement of the North's ancient problem were evident everywhere.

We stopped at Portadown, Newry, Dundalk and Drogheda to take on more supporters, and to receive good wishes from mayors and prominent local people. When the train came to a halt in Connolly Station the committee led the way along the platform to an amazing welcome. Chris Hudson and his team had done a wonderful job. The music of the Transport and General Workers' Union brass band echoed and resounded from the Victorian arched structure of the roof, and hundreds stood to welcome us beyond the barrier, in the station concourse. The Lord Mayor of Dublin, Councillor Sean Haughey, was waiting to greet us, but before we reached him Ken Maginnis, the genial Ulster Unionist MP, was mobbed by his Dublin admirers. It was lovely to watch.

Standing on the steps outside the station tea shop, looking over the happy crowd, nodding to acquaintances, including Proinsias de Rossa, the only begetter of the peace train, and smiling at my former colleagues from the *Irish Times* and the Dublin papers, I knew that this scene would have its day, and, like bigger set pieces, would soon be forgotten but not by me. At least this time I wasn't watching it on television and admiring others for standing up to be counted: I was spokesman for a unique form of protest against fascist tactics.

Just as the speeches began a little, elderly republican came up beside me and began to protest loudly about the closure of the border roads. I bent down, he looked up, 'Wheesht!' I said. 'The Lord Mayor of Dublin's going to talk.' He stopped with his mouth open, and nodded. Afterwards I listened to him politely; he was a Provo supporter to the bootlaces, but no bigot. When he'd finished, and he saw that I wasn't about to enter a debate, he turned to go. 'Good luck,' I said.

'Same to yourself,' he called back, in a ripe Dublin accent.

On the way back to Belfast, with the train crammed, we stopped at Newry and were not surprised to see a demonstration taking place on the platform, with people carrying boards and chanting about the border roads. I had advised those around me not to respond to republican chants at stations en route, but I should have used the train's public address system, because quite a shouting match ensued from some of the southern contingent. I was standing in the space between two carriages, looking out of an open window and shaking my head at the noise, when a demonstrator came exactly opposite me and stopped. We stared at each other for a moment. I winked at him. He shook his head sadly. 'I'm surprised at you, Sam,' he said, and walked away, leaving me to wonder how an otherwise reasonable-seeming man could possibly defend the blowing up of a railway line, or, indeed, any of the other forms of violence chosen by the Provos.

I remember walking the main street of Glenties during the Patrick Magill Festival one year with an otherwise peaceful and literate man from County Tyrone who truly believed that it made democratic sense to vote Sinn Féin whilst disapproving of IRA violence. Not for the first time, I realised that the Catholic experience in Northern Ireland must have burnt and rankled and possessed their very souls to a degree that no northern Protestant could possibly have imagined.

By the time the PTO was founded there were many movements for peace, and many good people to fill them. Some of them lasted, particularly those in which the churches were involved, but a great many faded and died, burnt out by the fierceness at the heart of the civil struggle. When organisations such as the PTO needed helpers who would stay the pace, it was no surprise that the numbers fell away after a couple of years. It was then that the people of the Republic, in particular Dublin, stepped in and charged the batteries of the war-weary northern peace workers with their natural vigour and enthusiasm. They packed committees, arranged thousands of signatures on petitions, filled peace trains and demonstrated against the paramilitaries of both sides in huge numbers. A young Dublin girl, Susan McHugh, rang an RTÉ radio programme in 1993 to protest at the murder by the IRA of two young boys in Warrington, Lancashire. She invited those who shared her outrage to come to O'Connell Street, in the heart of Dublin, to demonstrate their disgust and within an hour the street was black with protesters, but in my opinion, nothing in the whole course of the Troubles equalled the first march of the peace train supporters through Belfast.

It was an exhilarating moment for the peace workers of the North. This may have been a surprise to some, but it didn't surprise me. One of the delights of the Republic, for me, has been the way in which they support anything worth supporting, and celebrate anything worth celebrating. Their St Patrick's Day parades, unlike some in the USA, are totally apolitical and almost intoxicating to watch; leaving the spectacle of the parade to go home is like leaving the theatre after a fabulous play. The Irish citizen who wins a big sporting award is assured of a huge Dublin welcome, whether the victor is from the North or the South, Protestant or Catholic. I saw evidence of this warm-heartedness when, with the Republic of Ireland team out of the competition in Spain, Northern Ireland played in the finals of the 1982 soccer World Cup. I was in Spain covering Northern Ireland's games for the *Irish Times* and I learned from the news desk that the pubs all over the Republic were crammed with supporters, all yelling for Martin O'Neill, Gerry Armstrong and the rest of the players. When they won their way into the second round the empty streets outside the pubs echoed the excited cheers that followed Armstrong's winning goal.

When the Republic's soccer side played in the 2002 World Cup, the team's victories sent the *Sunday Independent* into the lyrical stratosphere with a front-page quote from Wordsworth which read, 'Bliss was it in that dawn to be alive ...' To understand this national behaviour fully it is only necessary to look up details in the southern papers of the grief and mourning that followed the death of the playwright John B. Keane, a wonderful, modest, gifted man of the people.

When that first peace train arrived in Central Station we marched through Belfast and the people cheered us along the way. Beside me were Pete St John, composer of the wonderful songs 'The Fields of Athenry' and 'The Rare Ould Times', Senator David Norris, Mary Banotti, MEP, Eamonn Dunphy and Tomás MacGiolla, then a Dublin councillor, later to be Lord Mayor. The Belfast stores gave the Republic's punt equal value with sterling, and the visitors homed in on the city centre. We were received at the City Hall by the Secretary of State, Peter Brooke, and when the time came to leave we waved our friends from the South goodbye on the peace train. On the way back the Provos handed us a propaganda scoop by phoning a bomb warning and stopping the train in Portadown station.

The IRA soon found that the top people of the Republic weren't as war-weary as the northerners. The most prominent figures on the train flatly refused to give in to the terrorists by taking the bus to Dundalk and boarding another train there. They stayed the night on the train, demanded that the line be cleared, and the press flocked to interview them. What must have been most galling to the IRA was the fact that Ken Maginnis went into Portadown and organised tea and sandwiches for the weary passengers through the local unionist party. In the morning I picked up Paddy Devlin and drove to Portadown and we kept the VIPs company until word came that the line was clear. When the train finally arrived in Dublin it was to a huge public welcome. This was later franked when Senator David Norris had heavy all-party Senate support for a motion condemning the IRA's action.

It was inevitable that the peace train would take on the kind of life that other movements had assumed before us. We took rooms in Peace House, the headquarters of the Peace People, the most highly organised peace movement in the North. We devised a constitution that was carefully worded in order to qualify for funding, we appointed Eileen Bell and June McClung as full-time workers, and other peace trains followed. Meanwhile some of our members joined other newly formed peace movements, one of whom, Families Against Intimidation and Terror (FAIT), opened its campaign by placing a man who had been ordered by the IRA to leave the country in a Catholic church and invoking the ancient right of sanctuary. I didn't like the idea, nor did Paddy Devlin. We had been grateful for the support of the Catholic Church in the North and we feared that our early support of FAIT might strain this link. We drove to the church, suffered the cold disapproval of the priest, sat helplessly while the FAIT supporters insisted on their form of protest. As Paddy and I left the church a car entering the grounds slowed to let us pass. Looking out from the rear of the car was Cardinal Daly. His glance was frosty. The sanctuary thing had nothing to do with us, but I turned and said to Paddy, 'There goes the Church,' and he nodded glumly.

So the years went by and the peace trains ran to Derry as well as to Dublin. We held on to support across the political parties and we obtained official backing from all the district councils in the North except those where the DUP were in the majority. The attacks on the rail line lessened, and, finally, the Provos gave the tactic up. Occasional bomb warnings continued to be phoned through, but they were mainly the work of freelance dissidents. The threat to the very existence of Northern Ireland Railways had been smothered. In our finest demonstration we brought a number of mayors from southern towns who were joined by mayors of Ulster towns in a march through the centre of Belfast to the City Hall, where, once again, the Lord Mayors of Dublin and Belfast shook hands.

We demonstrated outside the headquarters of the UDA on the Newtownards Road, and together with Seamus Lynch I attended funeral masses for victims of loyalist assassins, and continued to oppose the UVF, UDA and IRA in broadcasts.

One occasion stands out in my mind from those times: we were taking the peace train to London. When we arrived at Holyhead I noticed that Paddy Devlin was not taking the trip well; his diabetes had reached a serious stage. At Euston Station in London I decided to take Paddy home and miss the welcoming ceremony at Westminster. Chris or Michael McGimpsey, or indeed any of a dozen politicians present, could handle the situation. But before leaving for Heathrow I was delighted to see Gerry Fitt in the welcoming crowd. Included in the peace train party was David Bleakley, one of the strongest Labour leaders in the province, a Privy Councillor, and a former minister in the Sunningdale government. David, Gerry, Paddy and I took coffee in the station hotel for the hour before the main party left and we talked.

There is a singular satisfaction in one's pensionable years in sitting down in the company of people with good minds, who have put in good years, simply for the good of society. These three, Fitt, Devlin and Bleakley, had spent most of their lives fighting for justice and peace. That hour in Euston Station is among my sharpest memories. Things that we mentioned were nearly all might-have-beens, or if-onlys, but we had tried, upfront, to bring them about, we were still trying, and we could do no more. I only regretted that my position as a civil servant in a rank higher than clerk had meant, under the rules, that I'd had to do much work for the Labour Party covertly until I had left the service. Behind our voices, as we talked, were the repetitive chants of a group of Provo supporters, young people, with English voices, who in all probability had never seen the aftermath of a republican or loyalist no-warning bomb. Fitt and Devlin had suffered under the Sinn Féin and IRA version of reasoned opposition – armed attack on them and their families. Both Gerry and Paddy carried licensed revolvers in case they ran into any more examples of the same.

I saw Paddy home. In addition to the nausea and weakness of the disease that was killing him, he was beginning to show signs of the writer's nightmare – blindness.

For the three years from 1983 that formed the last half of my chairmanship of the PTO the administration of the thing took up a great deal of my time. Eileen Bell, who later became deputy leader of the Alliance Party and a member of the Northern Ireland Assembly, was a district councillor who had to keep her constituency work going as well as looking after the peace train office. She also went on to become involved in the negotiations that led to the Good Friday Agreement in 1998. The politicians who had been involved with the peace train in the beginning were up to their eyes in the deals that were to lead to the Agreement. I was trying to earn a living through BBC and RTÉ work, and my writing had been snuffed out completely, after a run of a book a year. PTO committee meetings were attended by only half a dozen loyal spirits, so, as soon as the first loyalist and IRA ceasefires were declared, I called other peace movements together in order to open a debate on where each body stood in the new situation.

We were asked by the central funding body to come and set out our estimates for the year. I announced frankly that the peace train had run a few stops beyond its useful life. I told the money men that we were going to disband. Surprise followed this. Ours was a peace movement that didn't want to get a life out of it; others had good reason to carry on. We were a single-issue movement, and the issue was no longer in doubt.

It had been an education. I'd had no idea until I found myself in the middle of it that the peace movement itself was a bit of a minefield, never mind the terrorists, although a much-reported clash among the Peace People years before should have warned me. Notwithstanding this, though, I had been privileged to meet hundreds of people who didn't appear on television, or travel to America to give talks, or have their pictures in the papers. They were the ones who gave counselling to the relatives of prisoners, comforted the victims of terror, made up parcels for prisoners, brought people together in community centres located near the peace lines. I had met police and prison officers who were mentally damaged by their contact with the lower reaches of terrorism, never mind those who had been physically maimed.

In this connection, during a visit to an English town in 1990 I had been greeted by a Belfast voice behind me as I was signing a hotel register. It was a young man of about twenty-two with his wife and child. He wanted to shake hands with me and I put my right hand out but he offered his left, because he had no right hand. He was a former RUC man and had lost it as the result of a booby trap bomb left by the IRA.

Within a day of my return to Belfast I was in a pub near Carlisle Circus, waiting for someone who was visiting a relation in Crumlin Road gaol. Behind me, face-down and sprawled across a table, was a young man of the same age as the RUC man. He was very much the worse for drink, although the pubs weren't long open. He was muttering to himself, a hero again, in the whispering world of the alcoholic. I glanced at him, then at the bar manager. 'Early at it,' I said, shaking my head, for I know more about the condition than is healthy to learn. 'Just out of the Maze,' the bar manager whispered. 'Did eight years. Political.'

Judging from the area we were in he could only have been an IRA 'volunteer'. I said no more to the man serving me, but I couldn't help thinking that both this lad and the maimed policeman were war-wounded soldiers. The glory days of service were over for them. They were spent cartridges. Then my friend arrived and we smiled and talked, quite normally, he using both hands to make a point, and I drinking coffee instead of cheap wine.

The peace train was really an exercise in which the

forces of reason and logic took on the IRA's press office. In our demonstration of the illogicality of bombing the railway line the Provos, hopefully, had been reminded that a wider principle had been established. Fifty miles – exactly half – of the journey between Belfast and Dublin by rail is in the Republic. Although the IRA regarded itself as a republican force, the people of the actual, living Republic of Ireland could work out their nationalism in civilised terms. They didn't need or want the help of Semtex to do so, and they showed it in their own principled way through ventures like the peace train.

In October 1995 I led a group of peace workers in the Forum for Peace and Reconciliation. Chris Hudson represented the PTO. Matt O'Dowd and David Grafton gave a paper entitled 'The People of Ireland' and Seamus McKendry's contribution concerned the Disappeared – victims of the IRA who had been killed and secretly buried by them.

Seamus's wife, Helen, had lost her mother, Jean McConville, in this way; the lies of Sinn Féin in denying IRA culpability in the murder and the slandering of the victim made Helen stand up to terrorist threats and demand to know the truth about her mother's murder. Jean McConville was an east Belfast Protestant who had married a Catholic, changed her religion to her husband's and given him ten children. She and her husband and family moved to west Belfast after suffering persecution at the hands of loyalists in east Belfast. In 1972 she was dragged screaming from her bath by republicans and shoved into a waiting car while her children looked on in hysterics. Jean disappeared, and Helen, together with her husband set out in 1976 to winkle out from the IRA the details of her mother's fate. In 1994 Helen founded the Families of the Disappeared Association, and eventually the Provos admitted killing Jean McConville, and added the names of other victims similarly murdered and buried. Details were given of some burial sites but only three out of twelve were found.

Chris Hudson and I had the honour of launching Seamus's book on the subject, entitled *Disappeared* and published by Blackwater Press in 2000, but five years earlier, in the Forum for Peace and Reconciliation in Dublin, Seamus McKendry's case was the most important of the three issues before it. The peace train and Matt O'Dowd's papers took minor places to this appalling chapter in the IRA's dirty war.

Chris Hudson had to take a good deal of flak from the Sinn Féin representatives around the table. Much more than myself, he was detested by the terrorists because he was from the Republic, carried the honourable flag of the trade union movement, was greatly respected by the people, and had a vocabulary and delivery that were lacking in any Sinn Féin spokesman of whatever level in the movement. The IRA's front men, as usual, took the line that to oppose the republican movement, by which they meant the violent wing of republicanism, was sufficient of itself to blitz an opponent's argument. Chris didn't need any help from me, but I sailed in anyway and reminded Sinn Féin that the peace train committee members had attended funerals of UVF and UDA victims, but of course they sat in silence.

Matt O'Dowd reminded the Forum that, historically, nationalism was more liberal than the line taken by present-day nationalists. Statements by writers from the early days of the Free State supported the view that the unionist people had the right to withdraw 'a territory of unspecified size from a republic within the Commonwealth', and that Father Flanagan, the chief ideologist for Sinn Féin in 1927, had said that there were two rights of self-determination on this island, and that the Protestant people had their rights.

The respected civil rights leader Paddy Joe McClean told the Forum that Sinn Féin had never explained why the rail line had been bombed, what it had achieved and why it had been called off. This led to the conclusion that it had never been justified and he congratulated the PTO for that. Francis Fitzgerald referred to my perspective over the previous twenty years regarding the sad failure of unionists to celebrate their Irishness, adding that I was presenting a discussion that day which challenged unionists and was a very important dimension.

Seamus McKendry's case, of course, was a complete embarrassment for Sinn Féin. Their representatives shifted in their seats, mouthed platitudes and were plainly relieved when the supporting speeches for the Families of the Disappeared finally came to an end and the luncheon break was announced. I was invited to join Sinn Féin at their table by Caoimhghín O'Caoláin, who was later to be the first of the modern Sinn Féiners to take a seat in the Dáil, and who had helped me with a travel book some years earlier. Caoimhghín appears to share my philosophy that the best way to understand an opponent is to show civility to him, and see what happens.

In 1993 I had a novel, *Touch & Go*, published. BBC Radio Four gave it a ten-minute segment and liked it very much. An American reviewer for the United States Library Association gave it an enthusiastic welcome, while a Belfast critic, unknown in the literary world but prominent in the peace movement, slammed it. Another critic picked up on a reference of mine – a dozen words or so – describing flowers that had seeded on top of a bomb-damaged wall, to describe the wartime air raids on Belfast as 'light', for his own dubious reasons. I challenged him but got no reply. Seven hundred were killed in the first raid in 1941, and another three hundred in the second. I know this because I was injured fighting a fire in the first air raid, then taken by ambulance to the Mater Hospital in Belfast. The best-selling writer Brian Moore, who was brought up near me on Clifton Street, described the scene in the Mater Hospital's casualty department graphically in his book *The Emperor of Ice Cream*. I was a part of that horror of dead and broken bodies until I was taken to a military hospital, where I was dug out of the wreckage when it was bombed three weeks later.

Ironically, one of the favourable reviews of the book came from IRA man Danny Morrison, who was serving time in gaol. Before giving it a healthy vote he was honest enough to admit that he had picked up the book prepared not to like it, no doubt because of the politics of the author. By that time he was writing novels himself.

Writing imposes a discipline and honesty of its own on the writer.

I was over in Hammersmith in London at this time, interviewing Maeve Binchy, when I got word that the acclaimed rock singer Van Morrison would like to meet me. I was given the address of a small café a couple of miles from Hammersmith and a time was agreed. I wouldn't have a lot of time, for I had a theatre date to meet, but I went anyway, and arrived outside the café to see the man himself peering anxiously through the window. He waved me to a seat and began to talk as soon as I arrived. I called a waitress and ordered a coffee and beef sandwich. It seemed that Van, an east Belfast Protestant, had been thinking about some of the things I had been saying publicly about nationality and culture. (I hope I have remembered the gist of what we said.) He listened carefully as I described how I had been born when the border was laid down, how our people in the North had just come out of an all-Ireland state, albeit one that was British-governed. In the loyalist district where I lived we would not have thought it offensive to be called Irish, and we wouldn't have seen the need to invent a culture that would show us as being different to the Irish in one half of the North plus those in the entire twenty-six counties.

In the ferment that had followed the Civil War I had heard my father say to my Catholic uncles that he was '100 per cent British', and I recalled seeing an old photograph taken during the Civil War of nearly all the people of our street, standing under a huge, decorated arch. The group included some men dressed in ill-fitting police uniforms: these would have been A or B Specials, many of whom had fought republicans along the border area, but up until the end of the 1920s we still felt Irish in ourselves. In our districts were children whose parents spoke with southern Irish accents: these were Protestants driven out of the twenty-six counties after independence. It took this, plus the dismissal by the cardinal of all the Protestant people of the world as un-Christian, to hasten the process in the early 1930s of unionist bigotry and discrimination against Catholics.

The Second World War drove out any anti-Catholic feelings I had. I enlisted in the RAF with a Catholic from the Falls Road called Paddy Johnston and we became friends. There were many Free State-born aircrew in the war and I felt closer to them than to the English.

We discussed Irish literature, Van Morrison and I, and he was very well versed in the subject. All through our talk I sensed that he was still searching for some formula, some key that would add confidence to his feelings about culture and nationality. I don't think that he found it in his talk with me. When I got up to go he thanked me. Despite some reports that he was difficult to deal with, I had found him to be thoroughly nice, although his Ulster thrift was still there. 'Oh, by the way,' he said, with a broad smile, as I was stepping into my taxi, 'you know that coffee and beef sandwich you had, well, it's all right, I'll pay for them.'

In the battlefield of north Belfast one of the greenest Sinn Féiners carries a surname that has pleasant resonances for me. The son is a republican, shaped and hardened by experience and environment, yet I knew his father well, and there wasn't an extremist corpuscle in his body. The father's name was Tommy. For all that I know, the Sinn Féiner concerned keeps it quiet that Tommy served in the armed forces of the Crown for the whole of the Second World War. He was called up with me to release regulars for the Korean War and during the couple of weeks when we were at Aldergrove we had many a lovely night out together, often ending up in Tommy's little house off York Street in Sailortown and eating hot soda farls just off the griddle, made by his gorgeous wife, Sal. It is impossible to think of Tommy and Sal as having extreme political leanings. I remember, in the late 1950s, he got into trouble with the manager of the factory where he worked because, at lunchtime in the canteen, he had pointed to the fish on offer and said loudly, 'Oh, God, Fenian steak. I forgot it was Friday.'

The Catholic lady assistant promptly reported him to the commanding officer. 'Why did you use that term?' the latter asked. 'Shouldn't you have known that it might upset a Catholic?'

'Well, it didn't upset me and I'm a Catholic too,' said Tommy.

I ran Tommy to earth in the same district in 1985. Sal had passed away a couple of years earlier. He was pleased to see me, but as he sat staring into a dying fire there was a kind of sad resignation about him. He who had been full of stories had none now to offer. His smile was a tired one. It wasn't just the long years that had stolen the laughter lines from around his mouth, it was the vicious war that had raged and bellowed at his front door and driven him out of his cosy, happy home into a bleak Housing Trust flat. His handshake when I left was limp and lifeless. As I walked away I wondered how many more of my generation on both sides of the divide were left sitting in front of their fires, empty of emotion. As if they hadn't suffered enough, having gone through air raids that had left five thousand homeless, never mind the daily casualty lists of the war, and the privation of the post-war years, without having to take sides in a murdering match that had sucked in their their sons and grandsons. I didn't mention his unforgiving son to Tommy, nor did he. It would have done neither of us any good.

I ran into John Hume, leader of the SDLP, all over the place. Inside and outside politics I regarded him in every way as a gentleman, but in fact I had been saying that whoever led the SDLP was bound to end up being hailed as a statesman, and captivating America. 'All that the nation-alists have had to do since 1969 was nothing,' I wrote, 'The unionists did their work for them.' I quoted David Bleakley, the Labour leader from the 1960s, who once said that if anybody were to take Northern Ireland out of the United Kingdom it would be the unionists. I said many times that the SDLP were decent and intelligent people, but they hadn't pulled off any kind of eureka feat in their political efforts. In his talks with Gerry Adams, which led to the ceasefire of 1995 and the Good Friday Accord, presumably Hume told the IRA that the unionists, hope-lessly divided, were money for jam, politically, something that many dismayed Protestants, imprisoned in political aspic, had known from the start. The Ulster Unionist Party (UUP) were bound and shackled by the Orange Order and the DUP. When it became clear that integration with Great Britain was not a runner, unionists should have rushed to mend fences with moderate nationalists. Instead, every yard of progress towards parity of opportunity for nationalists became a Stalingrad.

Hume's advice to Gerry Adams was spot on. Unionist ineptitude had brought about a situation where to be a republican in Northern Ireland was to hold all the high ground in the areas of fair play, political nous, common sense and even culture and the arts. John Healey's *Irish Times* column even hinted that Hume's fluency in French put him intellectually ahead of the unionist MEPs.

In Brussels I offered to John Hume my own vision of a Northern Ireland where Catholics and Protestants would be manifestly equal in all areas so that Catholics, comparing governments, would wish to stay in the UK, while retaining their Irish culture. A notional million Irish in Britain have chosen this option already, plus at least one-fifth of Catholics living in the North. I also mentioned West Germany's long years of yearning for the return of East Germany, and I wondered, in the light of the economic plunge that followed the fall of the Berlin Wall, how many would have voted the other way, if they'd known what was to happen.

John ended with his favourite French/German analogy: 'If these two peoples can sit down together and work in amity, after being enemies in two world wars, why can't we in Northern Ireland?' he asked.

As the world knows, the Germans talked peace only after their armed forces had been thrashed, their cities reduced to rubble, their war criminals tried and sentenced before an international court at Nuremberg, and after the USA picked the German people up and reminded them how real democracy worked. But I didn't bother to offer this view: John's a nice gentleman, but it would have bounced off his Appleton Layer and ricocheted back into some place like the Horn of Africa.

One evening in January 1996 I was chairing a meeting of the executive committee of the Irish Writers' Union in Parnell Square, Dublin, when I was called to the phone. The person at the other end was Fergus Finlay, an adviser to the Irish Labour Party. 'Would you consider running in a by-election for the Senate?' he asked. I was silent. 'Sean Fallon, the popular Cathaoirleach [Speaker] of the Senate has died,' Fergus continued, 'and the Labour, Democratic Left, Fine Gael and Green parties are prepared to back you, and you will get support from Independents.'

My head was having trouble taking this in. Of course, it was a wonderful compliment, especially when Fergus told me that I could expect the support of the Irish Congress of Trade Unions. I was a familiar enough figure in Dublin, I supposed, not that I ever attended swanky parties, press jaunts or gatherings of celebrities, and I was delighted that politicians in the Republic – and in the government, at that – had such faith in me, but what on earth would my own people think? I mean, a seat in the Republic's Upper House was a lot different from writing for the Dublin press or broadcasting for RTÉ. It might bother my family, who had for years been worried about the direction I had taken in politics, and most of all about some of the attacks made on me from both extremes. The family had been silent, once I had embarked on it, but this venture could easily lead to a plenary session, involving me, the wife and daughters.

And what about the loyalists? My home town was 98 per cent Protestant. It was one thing for them to give me a fool's pardon for being a socialist, and a writer with a head-the-ball claim to be Irish, but would running for the Senate of a country that many of them distrusted wipe out the pardon? Gordon Wilson, a northern Protestant, had accepted nomination for the Senate, but his was a different case, having lost a lovely daughter, slaughtered with ten others by an IRA bomb while at a religious war remembrance service. Gordon gained admiration throughout the island for publicly forgiving her murderers, but I was on no such lofty moral ground. This might look like taking the pieces of silver.

A year after the ceasefires, and after the peace train, I had left politics and gone back, with some relief, to general writing. This new development would place me in the cockpit again, albeit in the mannerly atmosphere of the Senate. It would certainly be interesting, though. If I were to gain the seat I would make history as the first person from the North to enter the Senate by way of a by-election. Since the State was formed, all other citizens of Northern Ireland who had been nominated for seats by various

Taoisigh had been Catholics, many of them members of the SDLP who tended to lie low on southern matters and say suitably nationalist things in the chamber. John Robb, a respected Protestant independent thinker, had served in the Senate as a nominee, but John's philosophy was somewhat removed from unionism's. In the end I couldn't resist the offer, having overcome my own criticism that it might look like the tawdry Paisleyite tactic of grabbing the privileges and claiming to fight for change from the inside. If I were to win, it would be the first opportunity for the southern parliament to take a close-up look at somebody from Belfast's working class who was Irish, yet preferred to stay under Westminster rule, and wasn't afraid to say so. More importantly, it would demonstrate to my co-religionists in the North the liberality of the then ruling Rainbow Government, as opposed to Fianna Fáil, the Republican Party, who would never in a million years have considered any such gesture, as I was to learn nineteen months later.

I phoned Fergus Finlay and accepted. The family just crossed their fingers and wished me luck. The news came over the wires an hour after my acceptance. Next day I learned that my opponent was to be Paddy O'Hanlon from County Armagh, one of the founder members of the SDLP. He had been out of the public eye for a number of years, but that didn't mean that he wouldn't be formidable competition. There was keen interest in the contest from the northern and southern media. I waited for waves from my neighbours and townies, but thank goodness, the only overt reaction was one of curiosity. It was probably the first time that the nice people of Comber had even thought about the Republic's version of the House of Lords. The man who filled my car up with petrol wanted to know how he would address me from now on. 'If Paddy O'Hanlon beats me in this election I don't want you to mention it at all,' I told him, 'and if I do win, I can't see anybody calling me anything but Sam, as usual.'

It was just then that my health took a dive. Between losing weight and energy I entered into the hustings in a fine mess, but the die was cast, and if there was dismay on the side of my backers at the sight of my drawn features they didn't show it. I went to the Oireachtas (Parliament), addressed meetings of the parliamentary parties supporting me, went around the offices and met TDs and senators in their working surroundings, and laid my curriculum vitae before them. They seemed satisfied. I was particularly pleased to learn that the university senators David Norris, Shane Ross and Mary Henry, and the Independent, Fergal Quinn, were my strong support- ers, as also were the Progressive Democrat senators, including John Dardis.

This lifted my spirits, but the graph went sharply downward when I was told that Paddy O'Hanlon was to be seen in the members' restaurant and the tearoom pressing the flesh wholesale. It gave me all sorts of pause. I had never been any good at the more upfront aspects of politics. I hated the notion of stopping people I'd never met before and asking them to vote for me, and I simply couldn't do it. Addressing whole groups in set-piece speeches was one thing, in fact, I liked it, but face-to-face pleading was another country. I hadn't the right nature for it. It was like stripping down for a fight only to see the opponent showing moves that could make me look like a novice.

I had actually met Paddy O'Hanlon before. He had won a short story competition run by the Arts Council of Northern Ireland in the mid-1980s and I had travelled with Michael Longley, the then literature officer of the Arts Council, and the novelist John Morrow to a village near Crossmaglen to present the award. Paddy wouldn't remember it, and I wasn't about to remind the public of it, in case it got him the literary vote. We went head-to-head on the radio and it warmed my heart to hear him ask whether I agreed that unionists should sit down with nationalists and talk about community government in the North.

'I not only agree that this should happen,' I said, 'I've been begging them to do it for years.' Paddy, like so many southerners, had obviously regarded me as an unrecon-structed unionist. I reminded him that I had been asking unionists to grant full parliamentary rights to nationalists ever since joining the Northern Ireland Labour Party in the early 1960s, although I differed from republicans and nationalists in that I hoped that this gesture by unionists would produce a Northern Ireland where the even break for Catholics would persuade them to stay under Westminster's much more efficient government.

Meanwhile, I was looking and feeling so wretched that a friend who drove me to Kildare Street to address more potential supporters pleaded with me to abandon the whole project and come under doctor's orders, but when I got up to speak I found a new energy and managed to press enough buttons to earn support. What helped me was I had learned that day that the Fianna Fáil leader, Bertie Ahern, had imposed the whip on the opposition parties; Fianna Fáil badly wanted to see me defeated and so this lent me more strength, I put everything I had into my media interviews. On those radio shows where the public were invited to comment I had received almost 100 per cent support, including, most interestingly, listeners from the border areas where support for IRA and Sinn Féin was strongest in the Republic. Since this could not have been because of support for my politics I took it to be the bonding influence of the sound of an Ulster voice that wasn't spouting bigotry.

On election day I went over in the Oireachtas and spoke to Paddy O'Hanlon directly for the first time and reminded him of the day I had handed him the prize for his short story. He responded with the civility that he had shown during all of the campaign. He was surrounded by SDLP and Fianna Fáil supporters, but I had my own comforters from the government side. On the day I had a majority of thirteen votes over O'Hanlon, which appears narrow, but under the rules of the election only TDs and senators vote, so it was a satisfying enough turnout, totalling 221 votes. As the result was announced I felt so weak that I was almost in dreamland. In my speech I forgot to thank the staff of the Senate Office for the way in which they had conducted the election, and although I did manage to acknowledge the courteous way in which the campaign had been conducted, I wish now that I had also expressed my frustration at having to talk tough over the years against the SDLP, a party made up of some of the most decent politicians in the country.

*

Shortly after entering the Senate I had to go into hospital. Fortunately the problem was remedied in a few days. I had been diagnosing and treating myself and making a bad stomach worse. Reinvigorated, I returned to my office in Kildare Street and was astonished at the amount of mail waiting for me, and it continued to arrive for weeks to come. One of the most prized letters was from Gerry Fitt, who had just lost his darling wife, Anne.

On the evening in the early 1960s when Gerry had won West Belfast for Republican Labour from the unionist candidate Jim Kilfedder – a good man, whose family had had to seek sanctuary in the North, fleeing from an anti-Protestant republican mob when Independence came in 1922 – and I had been canvassing in east Belfast for the Northern Ireland Labour candidate, Martin McBirney, who later became a judge and was to be murdered by the IRA. When word came through to us that Fitt was doing well against the sitting MP, we took our cars to west Belfast and ferried voters for Gerry. When his victory was announced the unionists present began to sing 'God Save the Queen', and I was happy to return Gerry's wink down at me from the platform. He had sailed under the merchant navy ensign, the Red Duster, on the perilous Russian convoys. He knew that I came from a family of seamen and that I recognised the irony that lay behind the singers' claim to loyalty.

I was moved to find that Gordon Wilson's widow wrote to congratulate me on my success. Mrs Wilson later sat in the visitors' gallery to hear me speak in the Senate. There was a nice note from John Robb. His voice had the true ring of the Ulster Protestant, in the tradition of 1798, and his public stand regarding the way to approach the Irish problem has been justified in part by the voting arrangements in the Assembly. Douglas Gageby also wrote to send congratulations, and to remind me that as a writer signing the book of Senate membership, my name was in a list which included that of W.B. Yeats.

One lady, Margaret Burch, from Newcastle in County Down, had read a story of mine in which I had praised 'The Divine Miss Davis', who taught the infants' class in my elementary school St Barnabas, on Duncairn Gardens. Miss Davis had given me a book during the war, and in reply I described my life and surroundings on an airfield in Bedfordshire in England. She wrote back in kindly terms about my writing, expressing surprise that the school had not acknowledged it by special teaching for advancement to grammar school. From 1940 until the end of the war I had posted little bulletins to Miss Davis, and on my leaves home she gave me the sort of advice that should have been offered by teachers of the more senior classes. Margaret Burch wrote that the Divine Miss Davis would have been very pleased to have seen my progress. When she passed on in the early 1950s, I lost my first true fan and mentor.

All told, I received over a hundred letters on my arrival in the Oireachtas. They included one abusive letter from a loyalist and a promise of an early death from a republican. I was glad to see both efforts – the bubble in the spirit level was dead centre.

As soon as the count and the television interviews were over I was taken to the Members' bar. This is a great privilege which I hold for life, together with entry to the Oireachtas facilities and the car park. Thanks to my love for horse racing, it wasn't long before I had a lots of friends. It's a great Masonic, the racing game: I feel sorry for those non-sporting northern senators who had, or have, to make their way in the Oireachtas without some sort of bond with other members, apart from politics. I was in the swim from the start, and politics have nothing to do with racing, so it was, and still is, a lovely experience.

I made many contributions in my nineteen-month stay as senator – probably far more in the short time I was there than any other northern nominee. The one for which I would most wish to be remembered exists in the *Official Report of the Seanad* for 12 March 1997. Events have rendered it redundant, but I doubt whether the Seanad had ever heard a speech like it before, or will again. Meantime, here are some extracts from speeches made by senators from all parties to welcome me on my first day in the Oireachtas, 28 February 1996. I include them here only to illustrate the cordiality that exists in the South for even-handed northern Protestants.

Maurice Manning, Leader of the House and a member of Fine Gael: 'On the first day of spring, and when the peace process is happily back on the rails, it is particularly significant that we have an opportunity to welcome Sam McAughtry as a member of Seanad Éireann. He comes from a community which should have a voice in this House. It is a voice which in the past was eloquently represented by John Robb and our late colleague Gordon Wilson. Senator McAughtry follows in a great tradition. We know he has an important contribution to make.'

Dr Mary Henry, an Independent: 'I have known and admired him so long, through the peace train movement, and his tremendous insight into a part of Northern Ireland which has not been represented here. We look forward to Senator McAughtry's contributions. I am sure they will be characterised by his wit, humour and sense of justice. If the debates prove somewhat tedious, perhaps he will read from one of his books, which are most informative about life in Northern Ireland ... perhaps the story of the Drunken Monk – it is about a horse.'

Jan O'Sullivan, a member of the Labour Party: 'He represents a strong tradition in Northern Ireland, which we are happy to have represented here. He speaks with honesty and wit and we look forward to hearing him address the House ... In the past twenty-four hours I have been somewhat concerned to hear the term "pan-nationalist front" being used by unionist leaders. Senator McAughtry will find that there is no pan-nationalist front: there are many views within nationalism, many views among members of this House, and many views among unionists. What we need is a spirit of coming together, trying to understand each other's point of view. We look forward to hearing Senator McAughtry's point of view.'

There were welcoming comments from nearly all the government and independent senators, and it was also nice to hear friendly speeches from G.V. Wright, the Leader of Fianna Fáil, and Michael O'Kennedy from the same party, the most experienced politician in the Senate and minister of several departments in past Fianna Fáil governments. I was feeling great. When a senator in front of me leant back to shake my hand I whispered to him, 'I could listen to this all day. I don't think I'll bother replying. It will only blow my cover.'

But eventually the time came when the kindly Senator Naughton in the Chair nodded to me. In my first speech to the Seanad I wanted not so much to create an impression there, as to earn the approval of my old friend Paddy Devlin, who had been so delighted to learn of my victory

184

in Dublin. He was seriously ill at his home in north Belfast,
hardly able to read or write any more, this man who had
loved so much to do both. He would be sitting that
evening, with his head bent towards the television, listening to *Today in the Oireachtas*, on RTÉ, and the tributes paid
to me, smiling, remembering all the tips he had given me
now that I was a politician. God bless him, he imagined
that I would be hurling myself into the arena, as he used to
do in his fiery prime, employing instant counter-weapons
to all challenges: 'Buy a wee transistor and turn it on every
half-hour for the news, Sam,' he'd advised. 'You want to
be in there first, every time. You don't want to be caught
on the hop.'

When I rose to speak I was thinking of all that had
happened to me since 1971. In nearly all the good things
that had pushed aside the bad, Dublin had been central.
Now I was next door to the pulse of its parliament. I had
opened my heart to Paddy Devlin. He was the only one I
had told of the connection between my progress in life
since 1971 and the affection offered to me by so many in
the Republic, a place that I was taught in the streets of
Tiger's Bay to fear.

'I thank you, a Cathaoirleach, and other Members for
your warm welcome,' I began. 'Someone said I am
expected to provide the unionist perspective. I am a
hybrid unionist in that I am happy to live in the United
Kingdom, but I am happier still to be Irish, and to
proclaim my Irishness. It is my dearest wish to see this
island inhabited by five million Irish people living in two
jurisdictions, with consent, but with institutions established to emphasise their Irishness. I have urged for some
time that we should negotiate as Irish to Irish. I am greatly
saddened to see graffiti on walls in my area with

references to the Irish as some sort of enemy. For people living in areas such as Ballyhackamore, to discourage the Irish language seems a sad error of judgement.

'As to my contribution to this House, there are certain things to which I shall make no contribution. For example, I am still attempting to work out the ramifications of the beef tribunal. I will leave such things to the government of the Republic.

'My background is Labour, and the issues that would interest a Labour man in any jurisdiction will interest me. I thank all who warmly greeted me. I am conscious of the friendliness I am shown on the streets of Dublin. I hope to travel around a good deal and to begin to learn about the process of government at the heart of democracy as it is demonstrated here. I live for the day when we in the North will also use pure democracy to run our lives, as people here do.'

One of the best-loved politicians in the Republic is Senator David Norris. He is one of the country's most dedicated public representatives. In a country like Ireland, with its narrowly religious background and history, it is not surprising that David should, in the past, have attracted more attention for his efforts in the European Court and elsewhere to lift the shadow of public disapproval from homosexuals like himself than for his marvellous work in the Senate, or the priceless contribution he has made to the preservation of Dublin's fine old buildings, or helping the public to appreciate James Joyce's classic writings. I once saw him in a dreadful BBC Northern Ireland television programme called *The Show*, where he was interviewed by David Dunseath. Davy Dunseath is a good broadcaster, but he was pulled down by the appallingly low horizon of the show. His opening words after introducing David were, 'David Norris, there are many people who would call you a pervert.'

Later, I was watching Norris being interviewed by a presenter called David Hanley on RTÉ and this time Hanley seemed to have a fixation with the notion of Norris having a lover in Israel. Hanley, too, is a fine broadcaster but it would seem the station demanded this. The synonym finder for the word 'pry' would seem to sum up the motive for it, viz. wrest, wring, wrench, dig up, root up, grub up.

Here is an example, both of David Norris's uniquely personal contributions to the Senate and of the almost village council level reached by Dáil and Senate debates. David had been complaining about young men urinating outside his door and I had interjected, saying that young men had always urinated in weird places.

'It would take a police force of a minimum of five hundred thousand to tackle this, because young men do not give notice that they will urinate at a given time or place.'

Mr Norris: 'If there were a few policemen at Fibber Magee's, P.J. McGrath's, Rumour's Nightclub and the back gate [of Trinity College] at these times, much of the problem would be solved. I cannot speak for Belfast, but I have no doubt that they urinate all over each other up there.'

I said something in reply but it had to fight its way through my laughter.

I remember Gerry Fitt telling me that there were quite a few peers and MPs fond of a bet on the horses, but I got the impression that they were regarded at Westminster as having a bit of the Artful Dodger about them. This certainly wasn't the case in the Oireachtas. In the Members' bar a typical racing discussion was on a high level of understanding, not just of form, but of breeding, training and administration.

I'm not sure, but I believe that I hold another record – that of the first northern senator to take adjournment time to mount a debate. The rules forbade a debate on the North, so my subject was the state of the Irish horse-racing industry. More often than not adjournment debates do not attract a great many speakers, so I was not surprised to note that, when I rose to open, there were only a few senators in the chamber. But as each of these drew near the end of his contribution he was replaced by a newcomer: clearly the debate was being watched on the monitors throughout the Oireachtas with a good deal of interest. As I was summing up after seeing the whole of the allotted time used constructively, Maurice Manning, the Leader of the House, came in and took his seat, and when he caught my eye he was beaming. On my first day in the Senate he had promised me the time and the debate, and now it had worked out splendidly. Horse racing is a great deal more than a group of animals running races and thousands of punters yelling them on: it is tied up with tourism, an export trade worth millions, and many hundreds of jobs. There are twenty-seven racecourses in Ireland and all senators, except perhaps those from Donegal, had race-courses in or near their constituencies; each had a point of view on the subject, and there hadn't been a chance to voice it for a long time.

My real pleasure, afterwards, was that I had taken an interest in a domestic, Republic matter. I wasn't just a disinterested northerner, in the House for a gesture. It wasn't my only contribution in this area, however, although my other comments were restricted to short speeches raised on the 'Order of Business'. During the BSE crisis in October 1996, I thanked the Republic's Minister of Agriculture for his help in emphasising the better health in Northern Ireland's cattle compared to British cattle.

When Sinn Féin's growing activities in unofficial policing against drug distributors came to light, I asked the House to have the primacy of the Garda Síochána emphasised through the Ministry of Justice. The Leader of the House confirmed that Garda responsibility was exclusive, and I was thanked for raising the issue. In the course of a speech in October 1996 on the growing evidence of the likelihood of the IRA committing an atrocity before declaring a ceasefire, I asked that an atrocity carried out in Northern Ireland be treated by the Republic as though it had been carried out in the twenty-six counties. This drew a quick response from Labour's Pat Magner to the effect that atrocities both North and South are condemned equally. This point arose in a debate some weeks later, the same response came back, but this time I said that it wasn't condemnation I was talking about, it was action.

In general, the novelty of my presence in the Seanad soon faded. One Fianna Fáil senator who seemed unable to accept my presence there, though, was the late Paddy Magowan, a hotelier and hard-working public representative from Donegal. Once, when I expressed concern at the way in which Fianna Fáil were claiming that they could handle crime prevention better than the sitting Coalition Government (a claim that looks laughable today) for this and for other comments of mine on domestic matters

Paddy complained to the Chair: 'Why is Senator Sam concerning himself with our business? I was under the impression that Senator Sam was here to comment on northern interests.' Later, in the tea room, Paddy, somewhat reluctantly, said, 'I'll admit that you're fairer than most unionists, but I don't see why you should vote in divisions over legislation that's got nothing to do with you or the Troubles.'

'It's because Fianna Fáil put the whip on against me,' I told him. 'Bringing me in here took guts on the government side, and not one of your party would entertain it, after bringing northern nationalists galore in for years. I'm as Irish as you are, but I'm more of a live, jumping Protestant than you've ever had here, so for the short time I'll be here you should try and put up with it.'

Paddy Devlin didn't agree with what I'd said. 'Paddy Magowan's a real gentleman,' my old friend objected. 'He was more than kind to me and my family at a time when we needed it.'

'Sure, as Fianna Fáil always say when they're pulling a stroke,' I said, 'it was only politics, Paddy.'

One of my last Seanad appearances was at its final sitting before the general election in 1997, when the government party lost to a Fianna Fáil/Progressive Democrats coalition. Senator Joe O'Toole, general secretary of the teachers' union INTO, and a trade union colleague whom I had long admired, said that it had been an extraordinarily useful Seanad, in terms of legislative work done. It was the first time in his ten years' membership of the House that ministers, because of the numbers in the House, had to listen to arguments and show flexibility and reason. I followed Joe with my final Seanad speech:

'I am glad of the opportunity to say a few words about my experience here. I have had a good many experiences in my lifetime. I have been lucky and unlucky. I have experienced many lows and highs. My experience here would certainly go down as one of the highest points of my life because of the hunger I have, coming from Northern Ireland, for democracy and all its aspects and benefits. This is what I have known here in the past fifteen months.

'I am full of admiration for those who nominated me for this post, but I wonder if they knew anything about me. I do not have a reputation for respecting the man in charge. I was like a fish out of water in the Northern Ireland civil service with all its hierarchical ranks, and the lickspittling that goes on in that sort of organisation in order to get on in life. I came here full of admiration that anyone would take a chance with me, not knowing what I was liable to say in the House. I spent the first six months watching, listening and lapping it up.

'We had a unionist government in Northern Ireland which was discredited for a number of reasons. However, the one good thing that could be said about it was that its ministers were accessible. That was a wonderful benefit, and those in the Oireachtas that hold the reins of power are accessible. This is true democracy.

'Three-quarters of a century have elapsed since Independence. The South has grown apart from the North. However, I have witnessed a bridge in terms of border colleagues who speak with the same voice as I do. I have been able to sit and reflect on history, and on what the future holds. I hope the future will hold good in Northern Ireland under the British government and this enlightened country.

'Despite comments I have made in support of my political views, I have enormous admiration for the way both sides in this House cooperate. I hope we will achieve full democracy in Northern Ireland similar to this State, and I hope the apparatus of law and order will be supported by all the people. I have enjoyed my stay in this House and thank Senators for the courtesy shown to me, and the true and warm friendship I have experienced.'

Senator Mick Lanigan, Fianna Fáil: '. . . Senator McAughtry has been a member of this House for fifteen months. I do not agree with his politics, but I agree with much of what he says. He has addressed this House in a reasonable manner, and I hope his time here has given him a better understanding of those who hold an opposing political view.'

Senator Shane Ross, Independent: 'I hope that was not Senator McAughtry's farewell speech. Let us hope he is back under whatever type of government is elected on 5 June . . .'

Senator Pascal Mooney, Fianna Fáil: 'My friend and colleague Senator Lanigan said he did not agree with Senator McAughtry's politics, but he admired much of what he said. The only difference between Senator McAughtry, Senator Lanigan, me and others is that we are Irish nationalists and he is an Irish unionist. Although that is a fundamental division, more unites us than divides us. My colleagues and I did not vote for Senator McAughtry but we have come to admire his fearless stand on many issues.

'He has said unpopular things, but he has also made points which needed to be made to inform and educate a southern nationalist electorate which has not always appreciated the genuine fears and concerns of the unionist community in Northern Ireland. If there is to be a political settlement on this island we must learn to understand and appreciate the concerns of that section of the population who will live among us, without compromising our basic beliefs and attitudes. I hope whatever administration is returned will ensure there is continued representation in the House of the two traditions in Northern Ireland. The House is enhanced and gifted by their presence.'

Senator Manning, Fine Gael: 'I ... agree with Senator Ross and everybody else in hoping that Senator McAughtry returns to this House after the election. All Members were impressed by his contribution this morning.'

After the election the *Irish Times*, in its Saturday edition, ran a piece by its Oireachtas columnist suggesting that if Bertie Ahern did not reappoint me to the Seanad as a Taoiseach's nominee it would not go down too well, in view of my record in the short time I had served in the Seanad. But Fianna Fáil, I had learned, hadn't a reputation of choosing statesmanship where party gain was the alternative. In the event, Ahern nominated as senators two northerners, Edward Haughey and Maurice Hayes, even though nationalism had an overwhelming majority already in the Seanad. Maurice Hayes insisted that he be allowed to take an independent line before he accepted the gift of a Senate seat, but in his first five years there he hadn't brought a frown to the face of any Fianna Fáil whip that I've noticed.

Well into the new session I was nominated by the Irish Congress of Trade Unions and by the leaders of all the opposition parties to oppose an almost unknown Fianna Fáil county councillor, a friend of one of the Independent TDs who were helping to keep the current coalition in existence. The Irish Congress of Trade Unions, four party leaders and several prominent literary figures attended a press conference in Dublin to launch my campaign. But it was a lost cause from the start, especially when the whip went on from Fianna Fáil, forcing their Progressive Democrat (PD) partners to do the same. Several PD parliamentary party members rang me to apologise for this, assuring me that, in a free vote, I would have had their support.

After the count I said in my few words that, as a trade unionist, I would always be proud that the Irish Congress of Trade Unions had named me for a Seanad vacancy, and equally proud that my campaign had been backed through a press conference attended by four eminent politicians, the leaders of the official opposition. 'I am proud of these things,' I said, 'but I am even prouder of the fact that, for the second time, Fianna Fáil has had to resort to the whip in opposing me.'

Afterwards, I was approached by several Fianna Fáil TDs and senators. They all had the same thing to say: 'It's only politics.' So it was, and I agreed with them, but, mind you, in any other circumstance, I believe that Fianna Fáil would still have opposed me. The other party leaders told me that Fianna Fáil would have fought just as hard against me if I'd been running for a place on the library committee of Dun Laoghaire County Council. It's not about secularism: it's about power.

In my time in the Senate there were a couple of debates that I remembered more than most. In May 1997, before making my final speech, I had asked that the peace process be kept out of the general election campaign. When Senator O'Kennedy commented that all parties backed the principle that there should be agreement between governments and the two sides in the North, I replied that it was the claim in the hustings that one side would deliver the peace better than the other to which I was referring. 'Britain has just been through the most vituperative election campaign this century,' I said. 'They tore each other apart with personal attacks, yet the bipartisan policy on the process remained rock-solid. Is there not a lesson for politicians here in that?'

I knew it would make no difference, especially to Fianna Fáil, who were making the claim, but I finished my plea by reminding them that the peace process was an attempt to cut down the killing on both sides, not an opportunity for politicians to build reputations. This was received in deadpan silence by the Fianna Fáil senators.

One debate in which I took part in February 1997 seized the attention of the papers. Senator Michael Mulcahy, a Fianna Fáil senator and a barrister by profession, was attacking in the chamber the bill which was the framework for the decommissioning of arms by paramilitaries. Decommissioning, he said, was as far off as ever because John Major had changed the goalposts following the IRA ceasefire. He did not believe that enemies for so long should lay down their arms in advance of what they saw as some kind of compromise. I rose, went into the chamber and received the nod from the Chair. Taking up my position, I said that Senator Mulcahy had just stated that he was a member of a republican party which opposed by constitutional means the right of the British to be in Northern Ireland.

'Well, I am British,' I told him. 'I intend to stay British, and I intend to work to keep Northern Ireland British. I am joined in this by nine hundred thousand northern Protestants and about two hundred thousand northern Catholics, the latter who, like myself, want to be Irish, but who want to remain under the United Kingdom form of government. It is no good senators saying that they are entirely opposed to violence, and then laying the blame for the violence that is happening wholly at the door of the British Prime Minister, while declining to condemn the IRA. During the ceasefire that organisation upgraded its preparedness for further war; individual members were blooded by killing petty criminals who deserved no more than six months in gaol.

'Mr Mulcahy has just said that the IRA exists for certain reasons. I thought that they existed to force me and people like me into a United Ireland.'

When I had finished, the senator stood up and denied hotly that he had any regard for the IRA and that he condemned their actions. Afterwards, we shared coffee in the Members' bar and guessed that we would both see our Seanad hopes get the chop in the general election, then we ended up chatting about common interests, which is the way it always should be. Michael Mulcahy became a TD and Lord Mayor of Dublin, and I remember him with fondness.

Dubliners are wonderfully generous contributors to good causes. There was a crisis in Romania in the mid-1990s and I decided to call into the charity shop on St Stephen's

Green and donate something. After me came a Dublin lady who lives near where I stay. Her name is Eileen. Her husband, Liam, had walked out on her some years earlier for a younger woman, leaving her without a penny.

Eileen is small and dainty, has high cheekbones and Russian eyes, likes colourful clothes, long dresses and long earrings. She flatly refused to take Liam to the law for a financial settlement, saying that it must have taken a great deal of courage for him to leave. Years after the break, she loved to reminisce about the days when she and Liam were teenage sweethearts together. The heartbreak would never leave her. With her family grown up and with their own responsibilities, she had had to go out to work to keep herself. In her late fifties, she had to accept low-paid jobs. From this work she earned enough to get by, but it was just enough. When she came into the charity shop and joined the queue beside me, we talked about the theatre, and the programme in the National Concert Hall, and the gossip doing the rounds among the regulars at the Dublin art galleries. When I was close to the counter Eileen explained that she had to rush to do her weekly meals-on-wheels run, so I invited her to take my place. 'I'm sorry it isn't more,' she said to the charity lady, as she handed over some money. 'God help them, out there: they haven't their sorrows to seek.' Then she left. It was my turn. Hurriedly, I added another fifty punts to the fifty in my hand, for Eileen, lovely Eileen, had given a hundred.

Listening to RTÉ radio one gets the full flavour of the post-colonial experience. Even though they're well on their way towards a century of independence, Dubliners still wear the status like newly-won Olympic medals. It fascinates me. In Cuba and around the Caribbean, it is necessary to remind the people of the revolution by huge hoardings and public monuments seemingly around every corner, but in Ireland independence is in the minds of the people, firm and fixed. The more that I visit Dublin the more I understand their pride, but I wouldn't imagine that many other northern Protestants would share that feeling. Such anti-British sentiment as exists has its origins in the fight for independence, and northern Protestants too often assume these sentiments to include themselves. But Dublin wouldn't be Dublin if they didn't go a little bit twee about it. Among my favourite memories is one in which Marion Finucane, presenter of a popular morning show on RTÉ radio, early in 2002, talking to an Irishman who had settled in Japan, asked him if the Japanese knew much about Ireland. 'Do they know that we've never colonised anywhere?' she asked.

I don't suppose the Isle of Man has either, come to think of it.

One day in April 1998, I was in my workroom when the phone rang. It was a spokesman for the National University of Ireland. 'Are you sitting down?' he asked. I told him yes. 'Well, get ready for this.' I was ready for some kind of take-off. 'I have just left a meeting of the University Senate,' he continued, 'and a motion to award you an Honorary Doctorate in Laws has just been passed. The Doctorate would be in recognition of your literary work and your contribution towards peace in Ireland.'

I put the phone down and sat staring at the computer screen.

When I first brought my family from the caravan in Millisle to Comber, after leaving the clinic, the man next door had stared, then laughed in disbelief when I told him over the garden fence that I was researching a book. It was five years later, at two o'clock one morning in 1976, that I wrote the last words in my first book and entered upon the nicest period of my life.

My brother Tommy and I served as combatants from 1939 to 1945; I enlisted and served with a Catholic from the Falls Road, and flew with men from the Free State; Dad and Mart sailed with Catholic shipmates, and my brother Tommy served with Catholic troopers in the North Irish Horse. For thirty years I had worked alongside Catholics in the Labour Party and the trade union movement. I was proud of this university honour, but I couldn't help smiling and shaking my head at this, the greatest contradiction in a life that was full of contradictions. It was one thing to wear glasses that neutralised orange and green, but this was something else. Once, in a County Donegal convent school, one of the nuns kept looking at me and smiling, as though at a secret joke. 'I'm sorry I was smiling,' she said, 'but I was wondering what they would say in Tiger's Bay if they could see you now.' After receiving this call from the National University of Ireland I was wondering what they would think in Tiger's Bay if they could see me gladly accepting an honour in the place where priests are made.

It was a beautiful day in Maynooth College, on 19 May 1998. The parchment was presented to me by the Vice-Chancellor, Dr Garrett Fitzgerald, a former Taoiseach, a statesman, an intellectual, and one of the sanest liberal voices in the Republic. Our Nobel Laureate, Seamus Heaney, was one of the guests. He and his talented wife, Marie, crossed the room before the luncheon to shake my hand. Out in the grounds, in brilliant sunlight, my three daughters, with their arms around me, posed for the papers; one daughter on each side of me, and one in front, just exactly as they had hugged me twenty-seven years earlier in the hospital ward. Those twenty-seven years represented one-third of my life. Add the years that preceded them and you have a life that at least ends with value added. I'm relieved and happy to settle for that.

Today I meet people of my own age who tell me that I'm looking great. They say it with a rising inflection, like, why aren't you clapped out like the rest of us? You're the same bloody generation, aren't you? Well, I know that some day time will get me, but the reason I'm on the go, living the life, peering at things closely and asking questions, is because I've lost so many years to idleness and sloth, the paralysis of ambition.

I can't say it enough times, in the welcome that I received in the Republic lies most of the credit for making this period a delightful dream. The doctors at the clinic started it when they took me out of the vicious circle and challenged me to go out of the door and make a new start in a city that looked as if its life was ending. The publishers of my first book carried it on. They were the ones who made it possible for me to have something to talk about on the radio. When the book was published I had the most delightful experience, meeting the people I'd grown up with in Tiger's Bay in bookshops, holding the book in their hands.

It is nice that my northern neighbours still hail me and josh me and give me the Belfast wink and nod of the head going past, despite my links with the Republic. I enjoy my life and make this clear. The North can be a sour, unforgiving place, but this is because of the actions of the disadvantaged at the edges of society, led on by politicians on both sides who have grown fat and prosperous by peddling fear. I don't believe that there is a people anywhere in the world more courteous and kind than those in the six counties of Northern Ireland. The nature of politics here has, over three-quarters of a century, been so virulent and so obnoxiously personal that the great majority want nothing to do with it. I have often said that I could form a better Stormont Executive from the passengers in the first-class carriage of the Enterprise express train to Dublin on any given day than the pick of all the governments at Stormont since the place was built.

There was never any need to lean on Catholics to ensure the maintenance of the British link and unionist fears led to blatant discrimination. Today, Catholics have achieved much more than the civil rights for which they fought in the 1960s. I hope it will mean that the comfortable Catholic will think twice before considering leaving the UK, but it is important to keep an eye on those lower-middle-class Protestants who are falling as silent as their Catholic counterparts once were. It is important to guard against the day when those who shouted loudest for civil rights for Catholics might need to do the same for Protestants.

It is not good politics to return humiliation with topspin. At a committee meeting I attended in 2001, after I had made a helpful contribution to a debate, a Catholic doctor beside me observed that I was an oxymoron, that rare bird, an intelligent Protestant. I think he meant it as a compliment, which makes it even more worrying. If, for example, nationalists are taking the Orange Order as representative of northern Protestant society they are gravely in error. Well over 95 per cent of Protestants wince as they watch such public relations disasters as the Order's insistence on marching at Drumcree and the Lower Ormeau Road. But there are no civilised routes through which they can enter moderate politics here, because moderate politics do not exist in sufficient degree, and the presence of the Orange Order in the UUP mix has added considerably to the problem. The merciless drubbing given to Labour candidates in the first Assembly election proves this point.

It pays no compliment to my political acumen that once, in 1994, I decided to try and bring the Democratic Unionist/Ulster Unionist parties closer together. I spoke to Ian Paisley Junior, who invited me to do my best. During a break at a meeting of the Irish Association, I raised the subject with a unionist councillor and a Belfast historian. The one glanced at the other and together, involuntarily, their eyes rolled. I respected their judgement and experience: that's when I aborted the whole notion. The DUP are specialist hecklers. That's all they can do. One of the best cartoons of the Troubles portrays Dr Paisley standing in a room holding a poster that says 'The Prime Minister Must Go', while beside him a civil servant is saying, 'But, Dr Paisley, you are the Prime Minister.'

*

In May 1994 I was part of a group from Ireland invited to take part in the annual conference of the Canadian Association of Irish Studies. My subject was 'Protestant Identity in Northern Ireland'. While I was there, staying in the pleasant surroundings of Erindale College, University of Toronto, two academics helped to put one important feature of Northern Ireland's problems into very clear perspective.

Dr Cecil Houston was Dean of the College. He came over to Toronto from Belfast as a boy when his family emigrated in the late 1960s. He and Dr Seamus Smyth were geographers. I was fascinated to learn that, some years previously, both men had carried out a survey of the Orange Order in Canada as part of a joint academic project. Nearly every northern Protestant of my generation would know that at one time the Order had great influence in parts of Canada. We would have seen evidence of it in the strong representation of Canadian lodges in the pre-war Belfast Twelfth demonstrations. There was extensive emigration to that part of the world at the turn of the last century, Protestants in general preferring Canada to the United States, at a guess, because of the strong Scots influence in Ontario. I was fascinated to learn how Orangeism had worked its way into so many aspects of public life in Ontario: the Twelfth of July was even a public holiday in Toronto, with an Orange parade as its chief attraction.

Jobs and favours could come out of the famous handshake. Since the geography and demography were so different from those in Ireland, Orangeism in Canada was smothered benignly by the vigour of the post-war multiracial Canadian population. Compared to the Northern Ireland of the late nineteenth and early twentieth centuries, Canada offered prospects to our emigrants which, if not as exciting as the dollar-crazy USA, still represented a considerable improvement in living and working conditions, as well as the peace of mind that came from living without the tension of cultures in collision.

I was taken by Cecil Houston to see the streets and houses where Protestants from Ballymena, Coleraine, Larne, Carrickfergus and Belfast came to live. They were tall roomy houses, in streets that were wide and in towns where there was space to breathe. Back home, these areas would have been considered lower middle class. On one of the main streets in Toronto I saw a building which is used as a leisure and community centre for Canadians of oriental origins. Above the door, and you have to look for it, chiselled in the soft stone, can still be seen the figure of King William of Orange on his horse. Cecil and Seamus told me that, on their travels, they had seen many such reminders of the lost empire of Orangeism, its two-and-a-half code talk and its secret sayings. If we in Ireland had not been so terrified of each other, this is how Orangeism and the violent republican response that it bred would have faded and died, sent into history by normality, until the last traces of both would have been of interest to nobody but geographers and historians.

As 2003 came in, on the unionist side particularly, there was an erosion of optimism about the future. At the time of the Iraq war I was constantly reminded by my Protestant friends that Tony Blair's attitude on disarmament by Saddam Hussein contrasted sharply with his attitude to the IRA. I was told heatedly that, whereas Hussein was punished for delaying his decommissioning, the IRA was rewarded handsomely for exactly the same chicanery. The mutual distaste felt by unionists and nationalists throughout the entire working-class population of Northern Ireland was palpable, eight years after the first ceasefire. Robin Wilson, in a paper co-written with Professor Rick Wilford for the Democratic Dialogue Group and published in early 2003, pinpointed flaws in the Belfast Agreement which actually entrench sectarianism. These include the either/or choice between the UK and a united Ireland; the requirement for Assembly members to register as either nationalist or unionist; and the method of appointment of the Executive of the Assembly. All points were well addressed in the paper but the first one mentioned is surely the greatest force for division, since, in the words of Wilson/Wilford, 'It does nothing to disentangle Protestants from unionism or Catholics from nationalism, hence the 2002 census results were treated like a sectarian rugby score: Protestants 53, Catholics 44.'

Do-it-yourself parliaments like Stormont will work for a while after a protracted political vacuum. All the parties will work together, but only in order to satisfy the politicians' craving for power, and for no other reason. The politicians are doing what they like to do, but their constituents have no such satisfaction. The mannered debates adopted by politicians in the chamber do not filter down to the disadvantaged Protestants and Catholics and the DUP use the tried and tested weapon of fear, feeding on IRA/Sinn Féin's unrealistic claim that a united Ireland is just around the corner.

At an event in Belfast's city hall in the autumn of 2002, Alec Maskey, an excellent Sinn Féin Lord Mayor, was honouring two legendary boxers, Freddie Gilroy and Johnny Caldwall. A boxing fan from west Belfast, in conversation with me about the game, surprised me by saying, totally out of context, 'My politics are different to yours.' It was the first time I have ever had to deal with a political statement by a boxing fan, and it shows how orange–green politics are contaminating community relations. The only sane solution lies in a move towards eventual left–right politics. Such natural politics, given the massive encouragement that would be necessary from Dublin and Westminster after eighty years of sectarian politics North and South, would certainly burn away the link between politics and religion.

As for me, I can close my eyes and measure to the last inch what navigators call the track made good. That story is a tale of one city. My voice is my Belfast visiting card, but Dublin is where I like to present it. I have met Dubliners on the meanest of streets and in swish Killiney mansions, I have seen them drugged on the pavements and I have seen them buying lovely works by their own artists. I have walked in Dublin's parks and along the Dodder river, where hawthorn and elder grow, bluebells and celandines, scarlet poppies and yellow ragwort, where dippers, wrens and herons fly, and where, in a field to one side, derelicts live, like badgers in setts, boiling the water of the Dodder in their kettles and telling me that the nuns, God be good to them, are very kind.

I first saw Dublin proper in Ringsend, the waterfront village so like the neighbourhood where I was born. There was a down-and-out northern Protestant there whose flat went on fire. The Ringsend people rescued him, got him a corporation flat and a job minding the door of the local pub, even though he was only five foot nothing and seven stone soaking wet. I learned about it from my great friend the late Lyrics Murphy, who kept records of Ringsend people's nicknames, and who made the thickest corned beef sandwiches in Ireland.

At the time of Dublin's millennium celebrations I loved Dorothy Cross for her mystical, illuminated boat, shimmering not far from where my father's and brother's ships used to tie up, near the North Wall. I greatly enjoy exercising my lifelong privilege to use the facilities of the Oireachtas and many there give me a kind word.

I have close friends in Dublin 4 who are Protestant, and I cherish this friendship. I only wish that some of my northern Protestant friends could understand that the relatively small number of Protestants in the Republic who have survived, despite the Catholic Church's disastrous mixed-marriage laws, are more genuinely and wholesomely and naturally Irish and loyal to their country, its culture and its flag, than all the grim-faced tricolour-waving republicans put together.

But anyway, to finish, I will always remember the lovely Dublin taxi driver who asked me, 'Are you the fella that tells the stories on a Sunday mornin'?' Arriving at RTÉ, he showed me a snapshot of his wife and himself, taken on holiday in a Boston park. Trees and shrubs, woven together, were behind them. 'Look close,' he said, 'and see if you notice anything.' I looked, and sure enough, there was something quare: a faint figure merged into an abstract background of leaves and tree trunks and branches; light and shade and slanting shadows. 'It's Our Lady,' he said. 'Look close. It's Our Lady, see? Isn't that something? Where would you get the like of it?'

Where indeed? But there you are, now. I'm not the only one who likes Dubliners.